Making Fairy Tale Scenes

Making Fairy Tale Scenes

Sybille Adolphi

Floris Books

Translated by Anna Cardwell
Photographs by Thomas Klink
Illustrations by Uta Böttcher

First published in German as *Im Märchenland*
by Verlag Freies Geistesleben in 2006
First published in English by Floris Books in 2009

© 2006 Verlag Freies Geistesleben & Urachhaus GmbH, Stuttgart
English version © Floris Books 2009

British Library CIP data available

ISBN 978-086315-718-9

Printed in Singapore

Contents

Introduction

I thought long and hard before writing a book about making fairy tale scenes. Fairy tales stimulate children's imaginations and occupy a very special place in their minds. One could say visual aids are not entirely necessary. On the other hand I felt it was essential to find creative ways of drawing attention to the old fairy tales, which, in particular the stories of the brothers Grimm, are so valuable for modern children.

These days many parents forget about traditional fairy tales, and if they are told to children they are often over analyzed. The joy of these wonderful stories is that they contain a great deal of wisdom, which children can absorb subconsciously without ruining the magic of the story.

Many children nowadays experience fairy tales through the medium of audio recordings. These are often amended or abridged; they come complete with background music to supposedly create atmosphere, and are read out by an unfamiliar voice. It used to be a totally different experience: the child would sit in a cosy corner, often on their parent's or grandparent's lap, a burning candle or roaring fire in the background and the warm voice of a known and loved grown-up relating the tale and transporting the child into the land of fairy tales.

In this book, I'll suggest ways to create a similar atmosphere for your children. You may find yourself inspired by the times you first heard fairy tales as a child, or you may simply be able to immerse yourself in a magical world that allows you to let go of everyday concerns.

You will need an edition of Grimm's fairy tales for telling the stories depicted in this book. (Details for *Favourite Grimm's Tales,* illustrated by Anastasiya Archipova, are provided at the back of the book. This collection contains the majority of the stories referred to.)

The projects in this book use a wide variety of techniques and materials for making the scenes. I have portrayed as many different fairy tale figures as possible, with various options for props. This allows you the flexibility to find your own preferred technique, be it with dolls, transparencies or wool pictures.

Once you have learned the basic techniques, you can use your imagination to make whatever scene you like from any fairy tale. You can also combine the craft techniques and figures as you please and, for example, make Rumpelstiltskin using dolls rather than as a transparency, using the gnomes described for Snow White and the Seven Dwarfs. Or you could make Hansel and Gretel as a transparency. All the fairy tales can be made as a wool picture, as described for Rapunzel. The trees, bases and decorations can be interchanged depending on your preference and available time.

Perhaps your favourite fairy tale isn't included in this book; the brothers Grimm wrote so many fairy tales, it was impossible to represent them all. I have tried to provide instructions for a broad variety of dolls, which can easily be transformed using different clothes and fabrics.

The dolls in this book are partially wet felted, partially dry felted. Most of the clothes are made out of felt or readily available fabrics like lace or velveteen. You can make the felt for the clothes yourself, and brief instructions on felting are provided in the chapter Basic Patterns and Techniques.

The patterns given throughout the book are to scale. All the fairy tale scenes are portable and can be placed wherever needed: in the sitting room or child's bedroom.

I hope you enjoy your creative craftwork, your storytelling and your experience of sharing these wonderful fairy tales with your child.

Using Fairy Tale Scenes with Children

In this chapter, I would like to explain how we as a family have used the fairy tale figures, pictures and settings. They meant a great deal to the children when they were still open to and eager for the world of fairy tales. This personal account is intended to stimulate your imagination and encourage you to develop your own ideas.

These small, hand-crafted fairy tale scenes were a special feature in our house. They were never used as toys; instead they were for looking at, lingering over and for illustrating the narration of the fairy tale. Of course the children already knew the fairy tales depicted, whether from nursery or home, but these visual settings complimented their favourite fairy tales and further stimulated their imagination. Naturally the children were allowed to place small items carefully into the scene, for example modelled animals or natural objects they'd collected. But they didn't normally remove the figures or play with them.

Our children put a lot of effort into helping to make the scenes, wherever possible, but I always made the fairy tale dolls alone. Then they could appear mysteriously, for example on a Sunday evening towards the end of our weekend together, or while on holiday, or for a birthday or during an illness. You will find many suitable occasions.

We attached particular importance to reading these old fairy tales word for word over several consecutive days or even weeks. You do not have to explain fairy tales to children or discuss their content or background. Fairy tales have their own emotional language that is intuitively picked up by the children.

They waited in anticipation for the figures, listened to the tales and observed the scenes, allowing them to unconsciously grasp the deeper meaning of the fairy tale. Rhythmic repetition of the fairy tales added to this. The children drew pictures, sang their own songs or acted out the fairy tales. They even celebrated fairy tale birthdays. Their experience of fairy tales was enhanced by their involvement in making the scenes.

This book shows both elaborate and simple fairy tale scenes, some requiring a large space and others that will fit in a small spot. What's important is that they are welcomed lovingly into the family and experienced as something special.

For more elaborate scenes, you don't have to set up the entire scene at once; you can build it up gradually. This enhances the excitement whenever anything new is added.

In our house fairy tales were connected with the seasons. While our children still enjoyed fairy tales (between the ages of three and eight), the same settings appeared time and again at the same time of year. Sometimes new decorations or figures joined the original scene. Such traditions, repeated over the years, give children a sense of security in our often fast-moving world.

In January or February, Mother Holle appeared in our window. With great excitement the children waited to see if she would make it snow outside too. Usually we read the fairy tale when the children came in from outside, freezing and tired from playing. We sat around the table with a cup of tea and watched Mother Holle shaking her feather downy outside in the natural world and inside in our fairy tale scene.

On the children's birthdays, we placed the Star Money fairy tale scene on the table in the evening once all the hustle and bustle had died down. We covered the scene with a silk cloth, which the birthday child was allowed to remove. The birthday child could also light the candles behind it. In this cosy and peaceful atmosphere we then read the birthday fairy tale Star Money. Afterwards, the birthday child was allowed to take the scene and figure to bed (without the candles!). By the next morning, the whole scene would have disappeared until the next birthday. Although our children are now older and have outgrown fairy tales, not a birthday passes when they don't fondly remember this tradition.

Our children helped to prepare the more elaborate scenes, such as Snow White, Hansel and Gretel and Sleeping Beauty. Together we made the background, the house, trees and so on, and then, with great joy, the children would see Hansel and Gretel appear while they slept; or we would bake the witches house together, and then the witch would appear in its doorway a few days later.

The children loved to see transparencies during darker times of the year, and so this technique grew as a new way of depicting fairy tale scenes. At dusk the children would light candles behind the transparencies, and everyone would look forward to sitting down together and reading the story after our evening meal.

We often made the wool pictures, such as Rapunzel, as presents for birthdays, the arrival of a new baby or a christening. Older children can also help make these pictures.

Basic Patterns and Techniques

This chapter explains the basic techniques needed to make the different fairy tale figures, of which wet and dry felting are the basis. As there are many craft books about felting, only the techniques needed to make the dolls in this book are explained.

The figures in this book are made using carded wool batting and magic wool (plant-dyed, unspun sheep's wool). Sheep's wool batting consists of many short fibres lying crosswise over each other in several layers. Usually the batting has not been carded completely smoothly, leaving some dirt and fibres in it. Remove these before using the batting.

A note about the materials: Throughout this book I have differentiated between 'felt' and 'craft felt'. By 'felt' I mean industrially made felt, sold by the metre or in sheets in a wide variety of colours. By 'craft felt' I mean handmade felt in sheets, softer than industrially made felt but with a limited choice of colours.

Needle-felting

Materials
Sheep's wool
Felting needle
Sponge or Styrofoam
Linen tea towel

Felting needles are available in three different sizes. Throughout this book I have worked with needle size 1.

Felting needles have tiny barbed hooks. These hooks felt the single wool fibres when pushed into and pulled out of the wool. You will need a soft base, for example a thick piece of Styrofoam or sponge. Place a linen tea towel over the base to stop the wool from felting on to it.

If you have never needle-felted before, I recommend making a piece of sample felt before attempting to felt a doll. This will allow you to see how the material responds. To make a sample piece, take a heart or star shaped cookie cutter, fill it with magic wool and felt the wool by continuously poking the needle up and down. Turn the piece of wool over repeatedly to stop the wool felting to the base.

You will soon see how easy it is to model and correct the shape, or decorate it by adding a few strands of different coloured wool.

You can also needle-felt around a Styrofoam egg or ball. First needle-felt one colour all around the shape. Don't poke the needle into the same place repeatedly or you will make holes in the Styrofoam. To decorate the egg, needle-felt patterns over the base colour.

Needle-felting is also used to add features to a doll after the body has been wet felted, such as a nose, chin, cheeks or bottom.

Needle-felting the doll's head

Materials
Skin-coloured wool batting
Felting needle no. 1
Felting mat

Weigh the amount of wool required. You will need approximately 5 g (1/6 oz) for a head with a circumference of 10 cm (4 in). Smaller heads need correspondingly less.

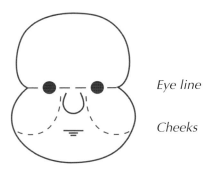

Eye line

Cheeks

Take the weighed piece of sheep's wool batting, pull it into a short strand and make a loose knot in the centre of the strand. Fold the ends of wool sticking out of the knot from the left and right over the knot to make a ball. Do not twist the ends while doing so.

Place the ball on to the felting mat. Poke the needle into the ball from all sides. This increasingly compresses the head. Continue in this way until the ball is the desired size and shape: this can be either round or oblong. Turn the ball repeatedly to ensure an even shape. Don't felt the head too hard or you won't be able to felt the eye line later on.

Felt the eye line into the front half of the head (see diagram for exact placing). Do this by poking the needle into the head repeatedly along the eye line to make an indented line.

If the surface texture of the head is too coarse for your liking, you can smooth it slightly by rolling the ball between the palms of your hand. If this does not suffice, you can further smooth the head by dipping it into hot soapy water (see instructions for wet felting, p13) and rolling it between your palms. If necessary, soap your hands first to make the ball easier to roll. It's important to rinse the head well in vinegar water after using soap, otherwise the soap will eventually cause the wool to corrode. Squeeze out excess water and place the ball on a tea towel to dry.

Wet felting

Materials
Soap
Carded sheep's wool/magic wool
Bowl
Hot water
Water with added vinegar
Base (e.g. tray or baking tray with bubble wrap)
Plant sprayer
Towels (to dry your hands between layers of
   wool, to absorb excess water and to dry the
   finished piece)

When wet felting the hot soapy water causes the scales of the wool fibres to open up. These scales then interlock when rubbed, making a compact material that cannot be loosened again.

If you have never wet felted before, it's advisable to make a sample project, for example, a small ball for a necklace, before attempting to make a head.

Note: Remember that all wet-felted objects shrink by approximately 30–40 per cent.

Put 1 tablespoon of soft soap into 1 litre of hand-hot water. Whisk the soap into the water. It's best to work at a sink or use a tray or baking tray as a base when felting.

Wet felting the doll's head

Materials
Skin-coloured sheep's wool batting
Hot soapy water
Base
Towel
Vinegar water

Weigh the amount of sheep's wool batting: approximately 5 g (1/6 oz) for a head approximately 10 cm (4 in) circumference; smaller heads use correspondingly less.

Pull the wool batting into a short strand and make a loose knot in the centre. Fold the ends sticking out the knot from the left and right over the knot to make a ball. Do not twist the strands of wool.

Immerse the ball in the soapy water. Very carefully squeeze the ball. Then let it glide from one hand to the other. This already makes it slightly more solid. Roll the ball round and round between your hands, very carefully and without pressure. Too much pressure will dent the ball. Soon the shapeless mass of wool will turn into a round ball.

When the ball is more stable — once the fibres of the outer layers have interlocked — continue to roll more vigorously until the ball is the correct size and shape (round or oblong). Don't felt the head too hard or you will not be able to felt the eye line.

Note: Remove any dents in the head by poking a sharp needle into the felt a few millimetres below the dent and pushing the felt outwards, or by felting a thin layer of sheep's wool over it.

Now make an eye line along the centre line of the head (see p.15 for exact placing). To do this, rub the back of a knife over the eye line repeatedly until you have an obvious indentation. Then use your fingertips to finish the line.

Rinse the head in vinegar water and place it on a towel to dry.

Making the face

Materials
Eyes: 2 small beads, or sewing thread, or a coloured pencil
Nose: Skin-coloured sheep's wool, felting needle
Mouth: Red sewing thread, or red magic wool for needle-felting on, or a coloured pencil
Hair: Hair-coloured sheep's or magic wool, or fake fur

Once the doll's head is dry you can start making the face following the step-by-step instructions below.

Nose
Take a small strand of wool using the same wool batting you used for the head. Tie a small tight knot into the centre of the strand. Place the knot just under the eye line where the nose should be. Spread the ends of the knot over the forehead and chin.

Needle-felt the loose ends firmly to the head until they have blended into the surrounding face. Needle-felt the nose into the shape you want.

Eyes
Mark the position of the eyes with two pins.

Note: Eyes that are too close together appear unfriendly.

Embroidered eyes

Coloured pencil eyes

Using a sharp pair of scissors, cut a hole into the centre of the base of the head for the neck. This hole should be large enough to fit two pipe cleaners twisted together and approximately. 1–1.5 cm (1/2 in) deep, depending on head size. Leave the pipe cleaners sticking in the hole. Cutting the hole now means you don't have to cut through the eye, nose or mouth threads later on.

Bead eyes

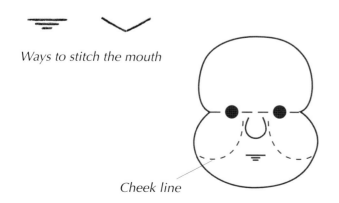

Ways to stitch the mouth

Cheek line

Using a strong thread (buttonhole thread or at least a double sewing thread), sew the end of the thread somewhere into the upper back of the head. Now push the needle through the head to come out at one of the pins for the eyes, pull the needle out, thread up one of the eye beads and then push the needle back the same way. Pull the thread tight. You can squeeze the head together slightly to do this. Sew in the thread at the back. Sew the second eye in the same way. Make sure you pull the threads tight enough to make eye sockets and don't leave the beads hanging loosely against the head.

If you don't like the idea of beads as eyes, you can sew the eye sockets without beads and then draw eyes with a moistened coloured pencil or embroider them on.

Mouth

Embroider the mouth by pushing a double, suitably coloured thread from the back of the head to the mouth position and stitching. You can embroider the mouth using either of the ways shown. Sew the thread in well at the back of the head.

Alternatively you can draw on a mouth with a moistened coloured pencil. Or you can needle-felt it on using a few thin strands of sheep's wool.

Note: a mouth that is too high can be mistaken for a nose.

Cheeks

Poke the felting needle in and out along the cheek line several times as shown in the diagram until you have made a small groove.

To colour the cheeks, draw red and some brown on to a small piece of cotton knit (using coloured pencils) and carefully dab it against the cheeks. Don't worry if the colour is too strong, it will quickly fade.

Chin (witch)
To make a pronounced chin, tie a knot into a thin strand of wool. Needle-felt the ends to the right and left of the knot to the head. Shape the chin with the felting needle.

Making the hair

Although I'm describing how to make the hair here, you should only make it once the doll is completely finished and dressed.

Sheep's-wool or curly-wool hair
To make long hair with a fringe, place a small strand of wool over the head facing the front. Sew it to the head with a few stitches. This strand will be the fringe. For the rest of the hair, lay a strand of wool from left to right, wide enough to cover the whole head, and sew it on with small stitches. If the stitches are visible, rub the needle back and forth over the hair so that they disappear under the wool. You can make braided hairstyles out of this wool.

If you prefer a centre parting for your doll, lay a small piece of cloth under the centre of the strand of hair wool and sew a straight seam with a sewing machine. Then fasten the strand of hair to the head with a few stitches.

For a shorter hairstyle use short-staple magic wool (unspun sheep's wool), shape it and sew it on to the head with a few stitches. You can usually still make short rat-tails or a bun with the ends.

If the hair is under a cap or a hat you can simply needle-felt it into place.

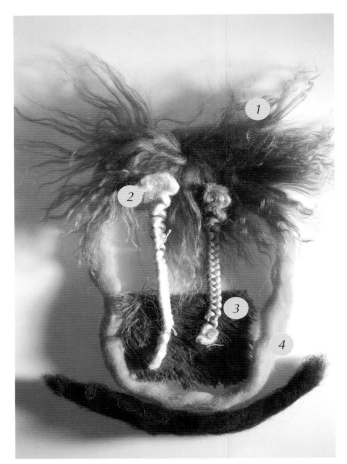

1. Long-haired fur
2. Curly wool
3. Short-haired fake fur
4. Sheep's or magic wool

Fake fur wig
Cut the wig out of fake fur following the pattern provided. Cut the lower edge slightly longer so that it will also fit a larger head.

Note: To cut fake fur, use a sharp pair of scissors and cut along the cloth under the fur so that the longer fur hair is not cut off.

Pin the wig together and put it on your doll. If it's too tight, you can stretch the fake fur. If it's too large, trim the lower edge. Sew the wig together and turn it right side out.

Now glue the wig to the head using craft glue. You can cut a fringe and/or plait the hair.

Making the body

Materials

Pipe cleaners (craft pipe cleaners are not strong enough)
Skin-coloured wool batting
Hot soapy water
Towel
Vinegar water

Basic frame

The body is made out of a basic pipe-cleaner frame wound with wool and then wet felted. To make this frame take three pipe cleaners, one for the arms and two for the legs.

Bend the arm pipe cleaner in half (see figure 1).

Twist together the top 1.5 cm (1/2 in) of the leg pipe cleaners, for smaller dolls less, depending on size. This piece is the neck, which will later be pushed into the head hole (see figure 2).

Put the leg and arm pipe cleaners together as shown in the photo (see figure 3). The bottom of the neck should be at the centre of the arm pipe cleaner.

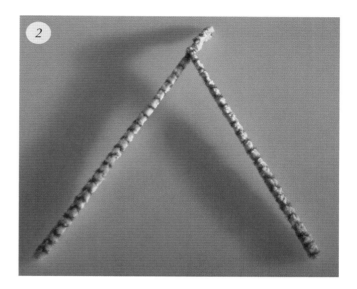

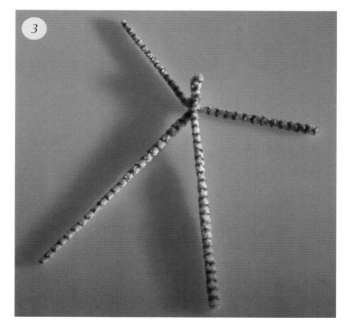

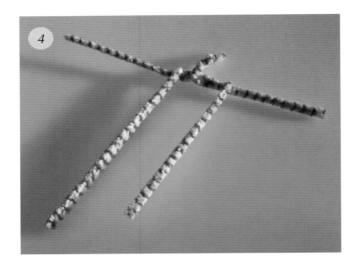

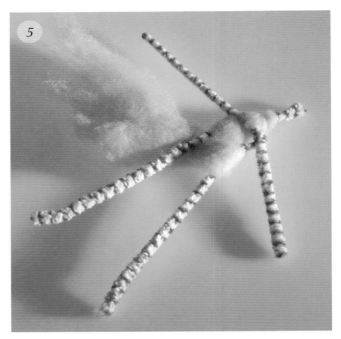

Winding wool around the body

Twist the leg pipe cleaners once around the arm pipe cleaner — right leg around the right arm, left leg around the left arm (see figure 4). This is now the basic frame.

Measure the required arm, leg and foot length according to the lengths given on p.23. Folding back the pipe cleaner ends makes rounder hands and feet and also prevents the sharp pipe cleaner tips from later poking through the felted wool.

Winding wool around the body

Wind strands of skin-coloured sheep's wool batting around the frame (see figure 5). Wind around the torso first. Start below the neck and wind the wool in a figure of eight around both pipe cleaners down to the start of the legs. Wind around the whole torso again once or twice.

Now wind around the arms and legs as tightly as possible without twisting the wool strand. It's best to use several thin strands wound around the limbs 2 or 3 times as this stops the sheep's wool

from slipping. Any uneven bits can be smoothed out later when felting. Only bend back the arms and legs once you have wound around everything, and then wind a thin strand of wool around hands and feet to make them slightly thicker then the rest.

Felting the body

Immerse the body in hot soapy water as described in the wet felting section. Put some soft soap into your hands and rub the doll carefully between your hands. As soon as the surface has compressed, you can start rubbing more vigorously to smooth out any uneven areas.

Rinse out the body in vinegar water, squeeze in a towel and leave to dry.

Note: Each doll is a slightly different size due to the different thickness of the strands of wool. Always measure the actual size of your doll before cutting out dresses, trousers or sleeve lengths. You do not need to add a seam allowance for the clothes patterns.

Joining the head and body and finishing

Remove the provisional pipe cleaners from the head and glue the twisted pipe-cleaner neck into the head hole using craft glue.

Wind a thin skin-coloured strand of wool between the head and body as a neck. If necessary, sew the head to the body first with a few stitches.

Needle-felt a bit of wool to the base of the back as a bottom.

Carefully needle-felt the soles of the feet straight.

If the stomach or any other part of the doll is too thin, you can correct it by needle-felting additional bits of wool on.

Shoes

If you don't want to sew separate shoes, you can wind shoe-coloured sheep's wool around the feet and felt it on while you are felting the rest of the body.

Patterns for making different kinds of shoes are given in the instructions for the different dolls.

Felting flat sheets

Materials
Hot soapy water
Soft soap
Spray bottle
Towel
Vinegar water
Base (baking tray or tray and bubble wrap)
Sheep's wool batting or magic wool

If you enjoy felting you can hand felt the clothes and shoes of the dolls as well as parts of the scenes, e.g. a carpet or meadow. You can also use leftover handmade pieces of felt to make shoes, flowers or gnomes.

Remember when placing the wool over the clothes pattern that the wool will shrink by approximately 30–40 per cent during felting.

Tear a bit of wool out of the batting, pull it apart into a thin layer and place it on to the bubble wrap on the baking tray. Place several of these thin layers down, overlapping like tiles, until you have the size you want. The fibres should all be lying in the same direction.

Add the next layer in the same way, but with the fibre direction at 90° to the previous layer, so that the layers are lying crosswise.

The amount of layers you need depends on how thick you want the finished felt. Make at least four layers. Everything else is dependant on the quality of the wool and the thickness of the layers. Once the wool is wetted you can press it down to assess how thick the finished felt sheet will be.

Now carefully spray hot soapy water over the wool. The wool should be wet through, but not soaked. Then soap your hands and carefully press the batting flat. If the wool sticks to your hands you have not used enough soap. If you are worried that you will shift the wool by pressing it too vigorously, you can place a piece of net curtain or bubble wrap over the wet wool. This will stop holes or thin areas developing, even if you rub too hard. After 3–4 minutes, remove the net curtain or bubble wrap and start stroking over the wet wool very carefully using circular movements.

Note: Remove surplus water by pouring it off every now and again. If your piece is too soapy, add some clear hot water. Too much water or soap prevents the wool from felting satisfactorily.

Once the wool has compressed lightly, carefully turn the felt over and repeat the process on the other side. The more the surface compresses, the more vigorously you can rub. Do not forget to work the edges.

Once the surface of both sides of felt has interlocked well, you can carefully scrunch and knead it. Then smooth the felt out again and roll it in a dry towel. Roll it back and forwards. Then proceed in the same way with the other edges. This process is called fulling.

Note: The more vigorously you full, the more the wool shrinks.

Once you have finished fulling the felt, rinse it in vinegar water, squeeze excess water out and leave it to dry.

Note: For a looser, softer felt used for clothing, do not full it.

Once the felt is dry you can start cutting out and sewing the clothes.

If the stitches are very visible after sewing the seams, carefully rub the needle back and forth over the surrounding felt so that the small felt hairs lie over the stitches and hide them.

You can also make grass for the fairy tale landscapes using this method of wet felting. The edges do not need to be straight, which gives a more lively finish. I recommend using at least 6 layers of sheep's wool. You can use different shades of green for each one.

Once your grass is finished, needle-felt a lake, path or flowers on to it. The possibilities are endless.

Note: If your first piece of felt has holes or thin parts, you can either carefully cut a piece off the edge and needle it to the back of the felt over the flaw, or you can needle a bit of magic wool over it.

Stitches

Gathering stitch
Gathering or tacking stitch is used for gathering cloth together, as the name suggests. To make a gathering seam push the needle in and out of the fabric at regular intervals. Then pull the thread tight to gather.

Running stitch
As with the gathering stitch, push the needle in and out of the fabric at regular intervals. But unlike the gathering stitch, do not pull the thread tight, simply sew the thread ends in well.

Backstitch
Backstitch is used for sewing two pieces of cloth together without the cloth gathering if the thread is pulled. To make a backstitch, push the needle through both the pieces of fabric to be sewn together, leave a gap the space of one stitch and then sew a backstitch that exactly meets the end of the last stitch.

Blanket stitch
To make a blanket stitch, push the needle from the back to the front and pull the thread through, leaving a small loop. Push the needle through this loop and pull the thread tight.

Mattress stitch
Use mattress stitch for invisible seams. Lay the two pieces of fabric beside each other with folded edges together. Push the needle through one layer of one piece of cloth, through to one layer of the other piece of cloth; now make a small stitch and push back through to the first piece of cloth, and pull tight.

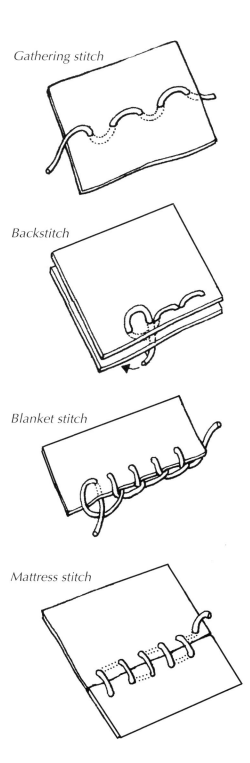

Gathering stitch

Backstitch

Blanket stitch

Mattress stitch

Doll Measurements

SNOW WHITE, SLEEPING BEAUTY, PRINCESS, CINDERELLA, LITTLE SISTER

Head circumference   9 cm (3 1/2 in)
Arm length   12 cm (4 3/4 in),
    including 0.5 cm (1/4 in) each side for folding
    back the hands
Torso length   4 cm (1 1/2 in)
Torso circumference   7 cm (2 3/4 in)
Leg length   5 cm (2 in)
Foot length   3 cm (1 1/4 in),
    including 1 cm (3/8 in) each side for folding
    back the feet

PRINCE, MOTHER HOLLE, WITCH, KING, QUEEN

Head circumference   10 cm (4 in)
Arm length   13 cm (5 1/8 in),
    including 0.5 cm (1/4 in) each side for folding
    back the hands
Torso length   4 cm (1 1/2 in)
Torso circumference   7 cm (2 3/4 in)
Leg length   5.5 cm (2 1/4 in)
Foot length   3 cm (1 1/4 in),
    including 1 cm (3/8 in) each side for folding
    back the feet

THUMBLING

Head circumference   6 cm (2 3/8 in)
Arm length   7.5 cm (3 in),
    including 0.5 cm (1/4 in) each side for folding
    back the hands
Torso length   3 cm (1 1/4 in)
Torso circumference   5 cm (2 in)
Leg length   4 cm (1 1/2 in)
Foot length   1.5 cm (1/2 in),
    including 0.5 cm (1/4 in) each side for folding
    back the feet

STAR MONEY, HANSEL, SNOW WHITE, ROSE RED

Head circumference   8 cm (3 1/8 in)
Arm length   11 cm (4 1/4 in),
    including 0.5 cm (1/4 in) each side for folding
    back the hands
Torso length   3.5 cm (1 3/8 in)
Torso circumference   6 cm (2 3/8 in)
Leg length   4.5 cm (1 3/4 in)
Foot length   2.5 cm (1 in),
    including 1 cm (3/8 in) each side for folding
    back the feet

GRETEL

Head circumference   7 cm (2 3/4 in)
Arm length   10 cm (4 in),
    including 0.5 cm (1/4 in) each side for folding
    back the hands
Torso length   3 cm (1 1/4 in)
Torso circumference   5.5 cm (2 1/4 in)
Leg length   4 cm (1 1/2 in)
Foot length   2.5 cm (1 in),
    including 1 cm (3/8 in) each side for folding
    back the feet

Spring

Cinderella

This fairy tale is particularly suited to spring, when the migratory birds return from their southern wintering grounds and start to build their nests. We hung the scene in the window to make it appear as if the birds were flying to Cinderella straight from outside.

I used a wooden frame as a surround for Cinderella. Discs of hollow tree trunk can sometimes be obtained from a forest ranger or from a market at a Waldorf School, or you could ask a woodwork teacher. Alternatively you could set the scene in a circle of plaited willow branches, for instructions see Mother Holle, p.77.

Another option is to use a cardboard box as a setting, with Cinderella and the birds picking up the lentils from the floor, instructions are given at the end of the chapter.

Materials

White felt for the underpants
Grey homemade or craft felt for the dress
Light yellow strand of wool for the hair
White and yellow beeswax for the doves and red and black beeswax for the other birds
Small bowl for the lentils
Lentils

FRAME SETTING

Hollow tree disc or willow circle
If desired kozo (handmade) paper for the background
String for hanging up

ROOM SETTING

White bottom of a shoebox for the room
Bird sand for the floor
Wood glue
Modelling clay with a 'granite' look for the oven
Small pot for the oven
Blue and green tissue paper
Coloured pencils

Cinderella

Make the body and head according to the basic instructions and measurements given.

Make Cinderella's hair using a yellow strand of wool.

Cut the dress out of craft or homemade felt, following the pattern. Sew the left and right side seams and then turn right side out. Smooth

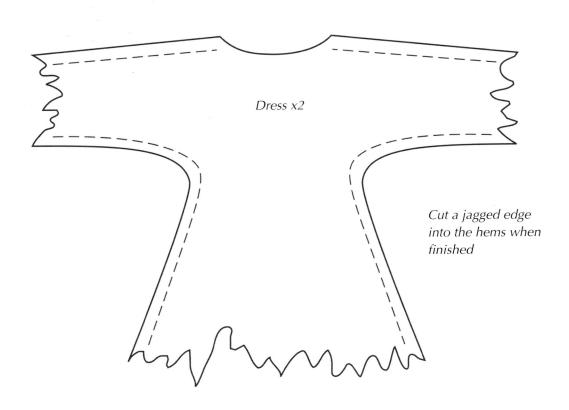

Dress x2

*Cut a jagged edge
into the hems when
finished*

the seams well with your fingernail. Sew some patches on to the dress to make it look old and worn. Put the dress on the doll and cut a jagged edge on the hem and sleeves to make them looked frayed. To finish, run a gathering thread around the neck opening, pull tight and sew the ends in well.

Doves
Model the doves using white beeswax. Make yellow beaks and use two black seed beads for eyes. You can model various kinds of birds using different beeswax colours.

Framed Cinderella

Cinderella is sitting in a disc of hollow tree trunk. Glue the birds to the wood using craft glue. If desired, you can glue kozo paper (or any handmade paper or tissue paper) to the back of the frame. The window in the background gives it a more open feeling.

Glue lentils into the small bowl and put it in Cinderella's hand or on her lap.

You can also glue some lentils around Cinderella for her and the doves to pick up.

Cinderella in a room

Cut off one of the shoebox's long sides. The other long side is the floor. Round off the top front corners.

Draw windows on to the back wall of the box. Cut out the windowpanes of both windows, cutting along the dotted lines as show in the pattern. To make the open window, cut along the upper arch, vertically down the centre line and along the bottom edge of the window as shown by the dotted lines in the second pattern. Paint the window frames and crossbars.

Cut the outdoor scene behind the window out of the blue tissue paper. Make sure the paper is cut slightly larger than the window itself so that it's easy to glue to the window frame. You can then glue green tissue paper fir tree tips to the back of the windows. Draw the flock of birds coming to help Cinderella on to the transparency behind the open windowpane with a wetted black pencil.

To finish, glue both of the backgrounds to the window holes from the back of the shoebox.

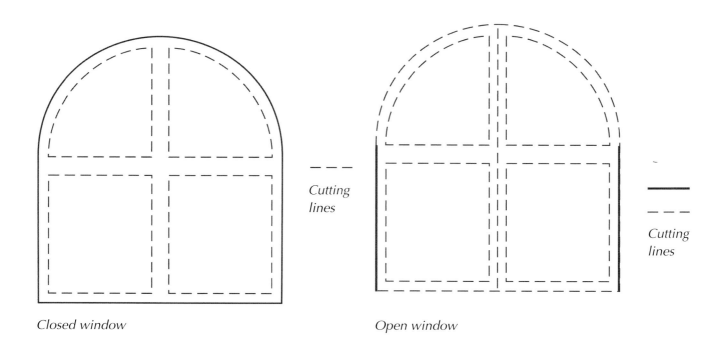

Closed window

Open window

Cutting lines

Cutting lines

Oven

Model a square oven using modelling clay. Cut a round space for the fireplace with a knife and smooth it with some water. Press the outlines of the stones into the oven using the blade of a knife. Now let the oven dry for 2–3 days or following the instructions on the packaging.

Make a bright fire in the hearth with yellow and red magic wool.

Floor

Coat the floor with wood glue and pour bird sand over it. Press the sand down well and let it dry. Place some stones on the floor while it's drying to stop the cardboard from warping. Once dry, pour the excess sand off. Spread some lentils over the floor for Cinderella and the birds to pick up.

If you put a candle behind the windows of this setting it gives a beautiful fairy tale atmosphere.

Snow White and Rose Red

There are many seasons represented in the fairy tale Snow White and Rose Red. However, the most impressive scene for our children was when Snow White and Rose Red met the little troublesome gnome on the meadow at the fallen tree trunk, and so we read this fairy tale between winter and spring. This is also the time of year when the winter coldness that the bear brings into Snow White and Rose Red's house is still well remembered.

For the setting I used an old wooden fruit box with the front side removed and painted a gentle green-yellow colour on the inside.

The gnome shown with its beard stuck in the tree trunk is one of the gnomes from Snow White and the Seven Dwarfs. Snow White is holding a piece of cut off gnome's beard in her hand.

As this is a fairly elaborate setting you can also build it up gradually, first putting Snow White and Rose Red on the meadow and then later adding the gnome and the tree trunk.

Snow White and Rose Red was a particularly popular fairy tale with our daughter and her friends. They enjoyed dressing up as the female characters, and even the boys were not averse to joining in as the gnome or the bear.

Materials

SNOW WHITE AND ROSE RED

White and red silk for the dresses

White and red felt for the dress tops

1 cm (3/8 in) wide elastic band for the underpants

Red velvet ribbon for Rose Red's hair band and
the belt

White satin ribbon for Snow White's hair band
and belt

Red and white magic wool for the roses on the
hair bands

White felt for Snow White's collar

White lace for Rose Red's collar

Black and light blond magic wool or fake fur for
the hair.

SETTING

Hot soapy water

Green sheep's wool for the meadow

Coloured magic wool for the flowers

Green magic wool for the blades of grass and stalks

Spray starch

Base (bubble wrap and a tray)

Towel

Paper covered florist's wire (you will need 30
wires, depending on the thickness of the tree)

Brown shades of magic wool

Snow White and Rose Red

Make the doll according to the basic pattern. For
exact measurements, see p.23.

DRESS

Snow White and Rose Red's dresses are identical
apart from the colour and collars. The instructions
below are for both dresses.

Cut the dress out of silk following the pattern.
Sew the side and sleeves seams. Cut into the
fabric under the arms 4–5 times to stop the seam
puckering. Now turn the dress right side out, iron
it if necessary and put it on the doll.

Run a gathering thread around the neck opening and wrists. Hem up the bottom edge of the
dress, or cut it to the right length.

Cut the top out of white of red felt. Sew the
sleeve seams. Turn the top right side out and put
it on the doll. Sew the back seam with a few
stitches.

To make underpants, see instructions for Hansel
and Gretel, p.67.

COLLARS

Make a white felt collar for Snow White. Cut the
collar out of white felt, lay it around the neck and
sew the back together with 2–3 stitches.

For Rose Red cut a small piece of leftover
lace and sew it at the back.

HAIR

Make the hair out of long blond fake fur for Snow
White, following the pattern provided. Use black
curly wool strands for Rose Red. For instructions,
see p.16.

HAIR BAND

Cut the hair band to fit around the head and sew
it together at the back. To make the roses on the
hair band, twist small bits of magic wool into
balls and fasten them to the hair band with small
stitches.

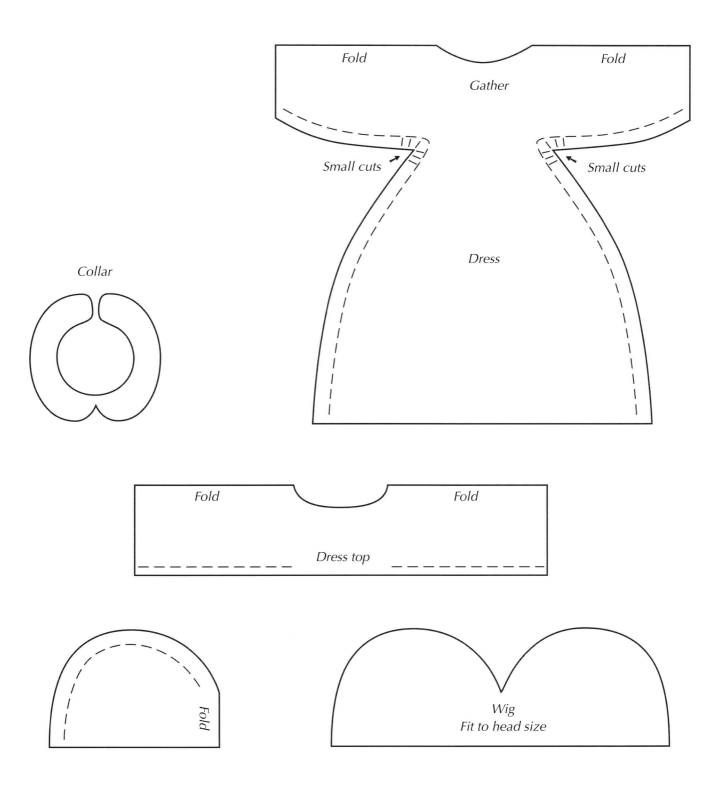

Fold

Fold

Gather

Small cuts

Small cuts

Dress

Collar

Fold

Fold

Dress top

Fold

Wig
Fit to head size

Setting

Meadow

The meadow is a felt mat made with 4 layers of wool. The flowers were needle-felted to it. The three dimensional plants in the background were first wet felted and then needle-felted on to the mat.

Flowers

Note: The flowers need to be very small to fit on the meadow. Only use a couple of fibres of wool for each one.

Shape the magic wool into a circle. Place a few fibres of a different colour in its centre. Spray soapy water on the fibres and carefully rub over them. Once the area has compressed, fold the flower over twice and lightly roll it back and forth. To finish, roll one end more vigorously, then, when you unfold the flower, it should have a nice chalice shape.

Note: If you cannot open up the flower again after rolling it, then the surface was not compressed sufficiently before you folded it. It can still be used as a bud.

BLADES OF GRASS AND STALKS

Place a thin strand of green magic wool on the bubble wrap. Spray soapy water over the wool and roll it carefully back and forth until it is firmly compressed. If possible, do not wet approximately 0.5 cm (1/4 in) of one end. This end can later be needle-felted to the meadow. The blade of grass/stalk will bend over if felted too loosely.

Needle-felt flowers to the tips of the stalks. Spread out the wool at the dry ends of the stalks/blades of grass and needle-felt them to the meadow.

TREE

Make the tree out of a wire frame using the paper covered florist's wire and then wind brown magic wool around it.

Take a bunch of wires of the same length. Twist them together three times approximately in the centre to make the trunk. Divide the wires at the bottom into 3–4 parts and twist each one together for the roots. Use wires sticking out the top to make the branches. Take three wires and twist them together. If the branches should split off further, separate off one of the wires and only twist it together with the others for a couple of twists.

The wire frame is now finished (see figure 1).

Wind brown magic wool tightly around the branches, starting at the trunk end. Once you reach the end of the branches, twist the magic wool lightly between your fingers. Then wind magic wool around the trunk and the roots (see figure 2).

If you want to use the tree for a different fairy tale and season, you can push small green bits of magic wool between the branches for leaves (see figure 3).

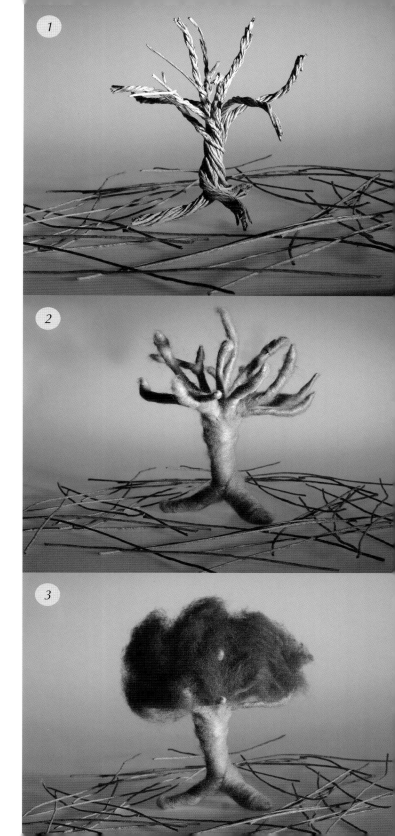

Rapunzel

It can be very attractive to depict a fairy tale scene in a wool picture. You can use these pictures as presents, or to hang beside the bed of a sick child while he recovers.

Rapunzel is the German name for rampion or lamb's lettuce, which plays an important part in this fairy tale. As the salad is harvested in winter and at the start of spring, we always read this fairy tale at that time of year. Our children were always motivated to eat their salad after listening to the fairy tale.

Materials
Felt sheet 38 x 58 cm (approximately 15 x 23 in)
Styrofoam for a felting mat (at least 2 cm/ 3/4 in thick)
Felting needle
Gold braid for the prince's crown
Magic wool in white, grey, brown, black, red, yellow, turquoise, skin colour, different shades of green, light brown, purple, pink, light yellow strand for the hair

For the background of this picture I used a handmade felt sheet — these can be purchased in most craft shops. They are not much more expensive than industrial felt, which is less suited to needle-felting as it's already very compressed and thus difficult to needle on to; felting needles easily break on it.

The Rapunzel turret is the most important feature in this picture. Start by shaping the white and red magic wool into a turret and roof and placing it on the base. Then loosely needle-felt the white and red wool to the background, which means only needle-felting it in some places. Do not compress the entire surface. Needle along the edges well to make the outlines clearly visible.

Follow this method for needle-felting all the objects and figures in the picture.

To make the stone outlines, pull the wool batting into thin long strands and needle-felt them irregularly but firmly to the base. This makes the stones appear more real as the loosely needle-felted white wool emerges slightly.

Now needle-felt the window shutters and the window for Rapunzel.

Put Rapunzel's head and body in the window and needle-felt them in place.

Plait Rapunzel's long braid separately using a light yellow strand of wool. Place the top piece of unplaited wool strand around Rapunzel's head as hair, and needle-felt it on well. Needle-felt the plait itself on loosely so that it still looks three-dimensional.

Now needle-felt the old woman trying to climb up the plait on top of the plait.

Next loosely needle on the path, meadow, bushes, fir tree and clouds, followed by the tree, the mushrooms, the bird and the prince.

You can carefully peel off any object or figure that didn't work out as you wanted and correct it.

To finish, sew a small piece of gold braid on the prince's head.

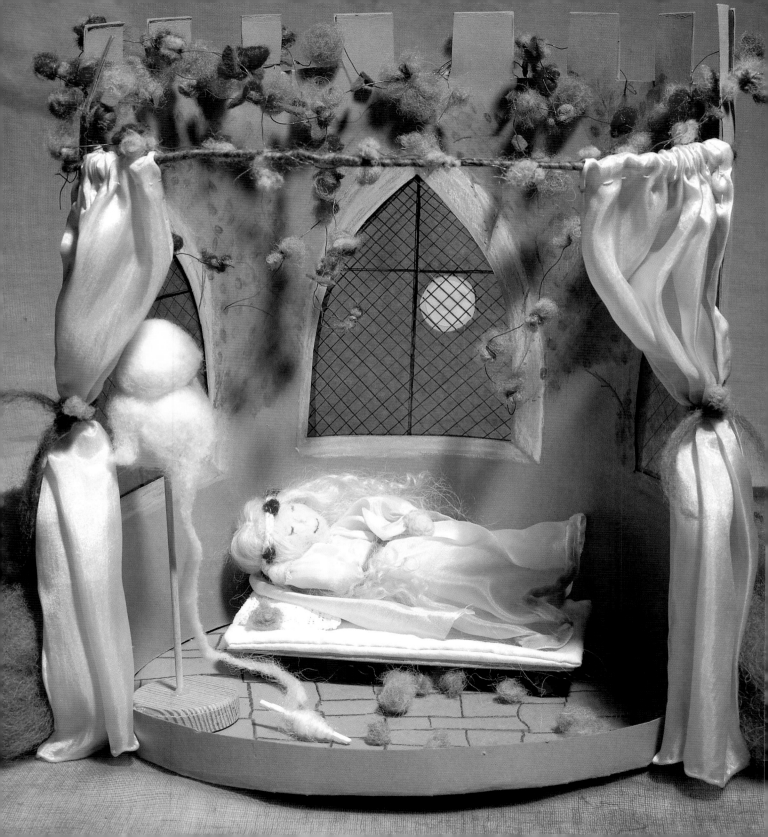

Summer

Sleeping Beauty (Little Briar-Rose)

With its blooming roses, Sleeping Beauty has always felt like a summer fairy tale to me. You can even use real rose buds to decorate the scene.

The setting for Sleeping Beauty is a castle made out of construction paper. A candle or tea light placed behind the windows in the evenings makes the scene look magically beautiful. The turret curtain can be opened and shut, which allows children to close the curtain once the fairy tale is finished and let Sleeping Beauty continue to sleep peacefully.

Towards the end of your time with this fairy tale scene, after you have read it many times, you could let the prince appear, cut through the rose hedge and finally kiss the princess awake.

Materials

SLEEPING BEAUTY
Pink silk
Velvet bands in different shades of pink
Pink sewing silk
Buttonhole or embroidery silk for the veil headband
Red or pink magic wool for the flowers on the headband
Curly blond wool for the hair
White felt for the underpants

PRINCE
Blue velveteen (if desired in different shades) for the shirt, trousers and cape
Blue felt for the over trousers

Black felt for the shoes
0.5 cm (1/4 in) wide gold braid for the crown and decorating the cape
1 cm (3/8 in) wide gold braid for the belt
Gold or silver cardboard or thick foil for the sword, or metallic paint

CASTLE SETTING
Grey construction (sugar) paper
Grey drawing paper
Dark blue tissue paper
Small piece of white tissue paper
Coloured pencils (if possible water soluble)
Black felt pen
Florist's tape
Silk for the curtains
Green sheep's wool for the bushes
Thin green wire
Red and green magic wool for the roses

SPINDLE
Wooden skewer
Small wooden disc
Unspun sheep's wool
Matchstick
Craft glue

BED
White cotton
Sheep's wool
Remnant of broderie anglaise
Small wooden or cardboard slat
4 wooden beads for the feet

Sleeping Beauty

Make the doll according to the basic pattern. For exact measurements see p.23.

Sleeping Beauty is the only fairy tale figure with closed eyes. To make them, fasten a double length of dark-brown sewing silk to the back of the head and push it from the back to the front, where the eyes should be. Sew a small vertical stitch for the closed eyes. Then needle-felt the eye sockets over it by poking the needle in and out along the eye line until the eyelids stick out three dimensionally.

For instructions to make her long hair, see Making the Hair, p.16.

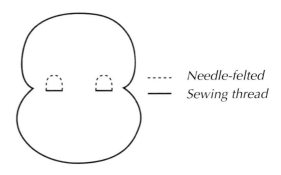

----- *Needle-felted*
—— *Sewing thread*

DRESS

Measure the exact length of your doll so that you do not make the dress too short. It should cover the feet when the doll is lying down. Remember the sash pulls the dress up further.

Cut the dress out of pink silk without seam allowance. Sew the side seams as shown in the pattern. Now cut into the fabric up to the seams under the arms 5–6 times. This stops the seam puckering. Turn the dress right side out and carefully iron it.

Now put the dress on. First sew the neck opening: fold back the silk to make a small hem and run a gathering stitch around this folded-back fabric. Then pull the thread until the neck opening is how you want it.

Make the sleeve edge in the same way.

Tie the velvet band under the arms as a sash.

Pin a thin velvet band to the dress hem and sew it tight with running stitch.

UNDERPANTS

For the underpants, cut a rectangle 13 x 5 cm (5 $^1/_8$ x 2 in) out of white felt. Fold the piece of felt as shown in the pattern (star on to star, circle on to circle etc.). Now cut into the centre of the bottom of the piece of felt as shown in the pattern. First sew the back seam using small blanket stitches, then sew the leg seam using small backstitches. Turn the underpants right side out and smooth out the seams well.

Run a gathering thread around the top and legs. Then put the underpants on the doll and push them up at the legs slightly. Pull the gathering threads tight and sew in the ends.

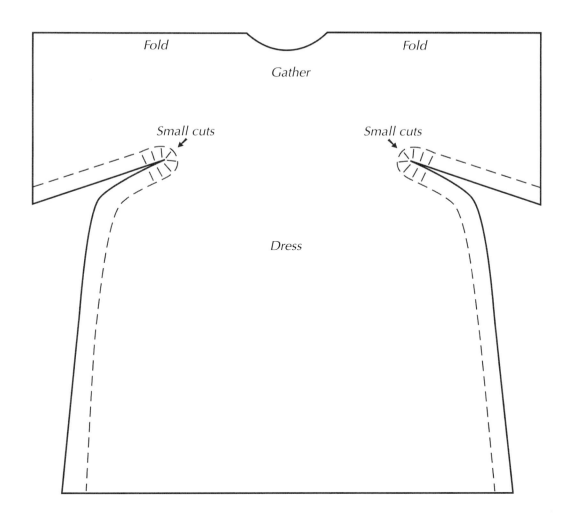

Fold   *Fold*

Gather

Small cuts   *Small cuts*

Dress

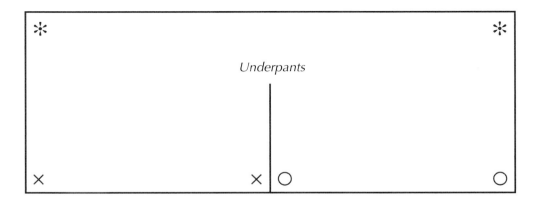

Underpants

Cut a piece of pink silk 17 x 22 cm (6 3/4 x 8 3/4 in) length x width. Hem the right and left sides. If possible the selvedge should be at the bottom of the veil.

Make a plait from buttonhole silk to fit around the head for a headband and sew it together at the back.

Gather the veil fabric so that it runs from ear to ear, as described for the neck opening. Now sew the veil to the plaited headband with small stitches.

To finish, twist some red or pink magic wool fibres into small balls and sew them around the headband as roses.

Sew the hair to the head with a few stitches and if necessary needle-felt it tight in several places. Place the veil headband on the doll's head.

Note: You can also make a larger version of this headband for your child, for the dressing up box or a birthday.

40

Prince

Make the doll according to the basic pattern. For exact measurements, see p.23.

TROUSERS

Make the trousers out of velveteen. The fabric will stretch when put on the doll and appear thinner. It is not necessary to hem velveteen as it doesn't fray.

Place the pattern on to the doubled velveteen, right sides together, and pin it tight. Velveteen is slightly difficult to sew, so I always sew it before cutting it out. Draw around the pattern with a pencil and then pin the fabric together outside this line. First sew the side seams. Then sew the inside seam.

Now cut the trousers out. Measure the leg length of the doll and if necessary shorten the trouser leg. Turn the trousers right side out and put them on the doll.

Run a gathering thread around the waist of the trousers and pull the trousers to the necessary width. Then sew in the gathering thread.

SHIRT

Fold the fabric with right sides facing and pin together. Then sew the side seams before cutting out. Cut the shirt out. Cut the fabric under the arms 4–5 times at right angles to the seam to stop the seam puckering. Now turn the shirt right side out and smooth the seams well with your thumb.

Put the shirt on the doll. Run a gathering thread around the neck, pull it tight and sew in the ends.

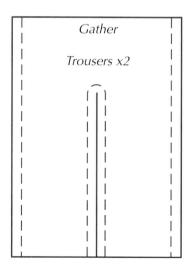

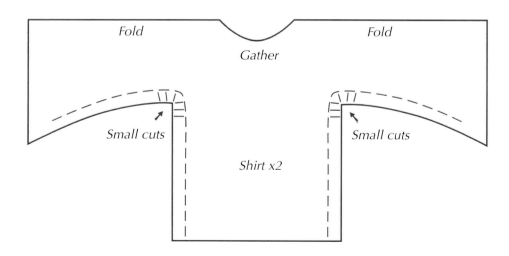

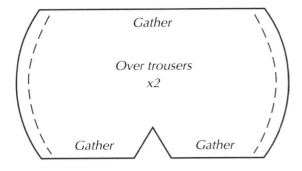

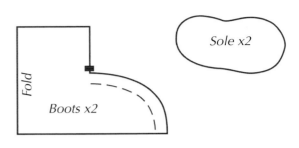

OVER TROUSERS

Cut two sets of the over trouser pattern out of felt. Sew the side seams and the centre seam together. Turn the trousers right side out and smooth the seams well.

Run a gathering thread around the top edge of the over trousers and the bottom of the legs. Now put the trousers on the doll. Tuck the shirt into the trousers. Pull the upper gathering thread tight and sew in the ends. Push both trouser legs up like knickerbockers. Now pull the bottom gathering threads tight.

To make the belt, use an approximately 1 cm (3/8 in) wide gold braid. Place it around the stomach of the doll and sew it together with 2 stitches. If necessary sew the belt to the waist with a few stitches so that it doesn't slip.

CAPE

Cut a rectangle 10 x 21 cm (4 x 8 1/4 in) out of velveteen.

To make the collar, cut a 2 x 21 cm (3/4 x 8 1/4 in) rectangle out of the same fabric. Glue a

0.5 cm (1/4 in) wide gold braid to the wrong side (inside) of the collar. Now lay both rectangles over each other so that the velvet side is visible on the cape, and the inside with the gold braid is visible on the collar. Run a gathering thread around the top edges of the two fabrics to sew them together. Pull the gathering thread so that the cape can be closed at the front.

You can either sew the cape to the doll or make a catch using a bead and an eyelet. Bead and eyelet have the advantage that you can take off the cape if you want to use the prince for a different fairy tale.

To finish, cut the two armholes into the correct places and push the arms through the cape.

BOOTS

Cut the soles and shafts of the boot out of black felt. Sew the upper half of the shaft up to the marked place, left side to left side together. Pin the sole to the shaft starting at the heel (if necessary tack it too). Now sew the pieces together. Make the second boot in the same way.

Turn the boot right side out and put it on the doll. Sew the upper part of the shaft shut with cross stitches to make it look like it's laced. Alternatively you could glue the corners of the shaft down to the left and right.

CROWN AND SWORD

Fasten a 0.5 cm (¹/₄ in) wide gold braid to the doll's head.

Cut the sword out of firm gold/silver cardboard or foil, or paint it gold or silver.

Sword

Setting

SPINDLE

Drill a hole into the centre of the wooden disc, diameter the size of the wooden skewer. Shorten the stick to the desired length and glue it into the hole. Let it dry well.

Attach a bit of wool to the top of the wooden stick by gluing it on lightly. Then wind a thin

piece of sheep's wool yarn around the lower third and knot it tight. This sheep's wool yarn can be long enough to wind around the matchstick (see picture) too. The matchstick is the actual spindle.

To finish, pluck the wool into the desired shape.

BED

Use a piece of wood or cardboard 7 x 14 cm (2 $3/4$ x 5 $1/2$ in) for the bed itself. If you use a wooden board, sand the edges smooth. Glue a wooden bead to each of the four corners to make the feet of the bed.

To make the pillow, cut a piece of white broderie anglaise 4 x 10 cm (1 $1/2$ x 4 in) and fold it in half. Sew the edges together with running stitch. Before completely closing the pillow, stuff it with some sheep's wool.

To make the mattress, cut two pieces of white cotton fabric, each 15 x 8 cm (6 x 3 $1/4$ in). Sew three sides of the pieces together with backstitch, 0.5 cm ($1/4$ in) away from the edge. Turn it right side out and iron. If you want you can stuff the mattress lightly with sheep's wool. To finish, sew the open side with blanket stitches.

CASTLE

Cut a rectangle out of grey construction paper, 27 cm (10 $1/2$ in) high and 44 cm (17 $1/4$ in) wide. This rectangle is the turret wall of Sleeping Beauty's fairy tale castle.

Sketch the pinnacles to the top edge and cut them out. Sketch three windows on to the castle wall using the window templates given and then cut them out. Remember the distance between the lower edge of the paper and the lower edge of the window is approximately 8 cm (3 $1/8$ in).

Place the construction paper underneath the drawing paper and trace the windows on to the drawing paper. Then cut these out too. The drawing paper will become the back of the castle, covering the glued bits of tissue paper.

Draw around the outline of the window on the inside of the castle scene to make the windows look more three-dimensional. Now draw on the climbing roses and leaves. I recommend using water-soluble pencils for this. Use the water sparingly so that the cardboard doesn't warp. You could use any kind of coloured pencils or wax crayons.

Glue blue tissue paper behind the windows. To make the moon, cut a round hole into one of the window transparencies. Glue white tissue paper behind the hole. Glue a second, smaller circle of white tissue paper on to the first piece. Draw the window cross bar and the lattice with a black felt tip pen (see window template).

Glue the drawing paper to the back of the construction paper.

To make the floor, cut a strip out of grey construction paper, 68 cm (26 $3/4$ in) long and 5 cm (2 in) wide. Divide the 5 cm (2 in) side into 2 ($3/4$ in) and 3 cm (1 $1/4$ in) with a pencil line. Fold the paper along this line. If necessary, score along the line first to make it easier to fold. Along the 3 cm (1 $1/4$ in) side, cut into the construction paper every 0.5 cm ($1/4$ in) up to the fold line. Bend the strip into a circle and staple the ends together. Glue a construction-paper circle, radius 10.8 cm (4 $1/4$ in), to the cut-in side. Draw an irregular stone pattern over the circle with a black felt-tip pen before gluing it in place.

Glue the turret wall to the floor. To do this, coat the inside edge of the floor border with craft glue. The edges of the wall can also be stapled at the left and right.

Make two small holes approximately 1 cm ($3/8$

in) away from the left and the right top edges. To keep the tops of the wall stable, a wire wound with green magic wool is later pulled through and attached. Put the curtain on to the wire first!

Cut two rectangles out of silk, 25 cm (9 ³/4 in) wide and 21 cm (8 ¹/4 cm) long. Measure the exact length of your castle first. Fold the top edge over, wide enough for the wire to fit through easily. Hem it with small running stitches. Hem all the edges of the curtain.

Fasten the wire through the holes in the castle walls and secure. Draw back the curtains to the left and right sides and tie them with wool yarn or a twisted cord. The curtains can be opened and shut as you please. Some children like it when the curtains are closed after the fairy tale is finished so that Sleeping Beauty can continue sleeping in peace.

Pull out small bits of pink wool to make the rose trellises around the castle. Wind green wool around the bottom of them tightly to cover the flower like a calyx. If necessary you can fasten the flowers to the calyx by poking the felting needle through them a few times.

Take a green piece of florist's wire, any length you want. Wind the flowers one by one around it by the calyx (wind the wire around the calyx 1 to 2 times). Decorate the castle wall with this flower chain.

Make the bushes at the sides of the castle out of loosely-teased green magic wool. Lightly needle-felt them into shape.

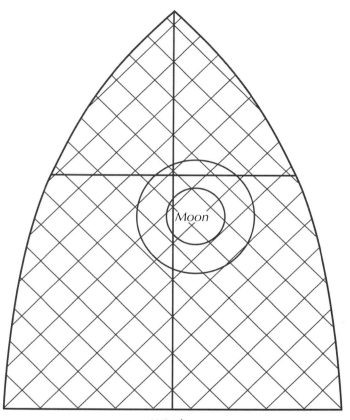

Window

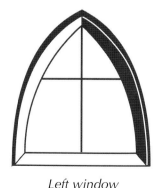

Left window

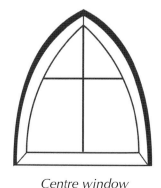

Centre window

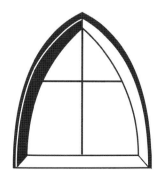

Right window

45

Autumn

Thumbling

I chose this fairy tale because the children always thought it very sweet that Thumbling is small enough to sleep in a snail shell.

This setting is also very small and fits on a dining table. Make the settings as you wish using wood, twigs, flowers and autumn fruits.

Sometimes when I told this story to the children, Thumbling would leave his snail's house during the day to go and sit on the tree trunk. He would then creep back into his snail's shell in the evening while we read the fairy tale and sleep by the light of a candle or the moon, dreaming of his great adventure.

Materials

THUMBLING
Green and brown felt
Brown magic wool for the hair
Wool yarn for the belt

SNAIL SHELL
Magic wool batting the colour of the snail shell,
 approximately 27 x 27 cm (10 $1/2$ x 10 $1/2$ in)
Felting needle
Felting mat

Snail shell

Wool batting is made up of many thin layers. Carefully tease them apart lengthwise. The thinner and more even the separate layers are, the easier it is to work with them later (see figure 1).

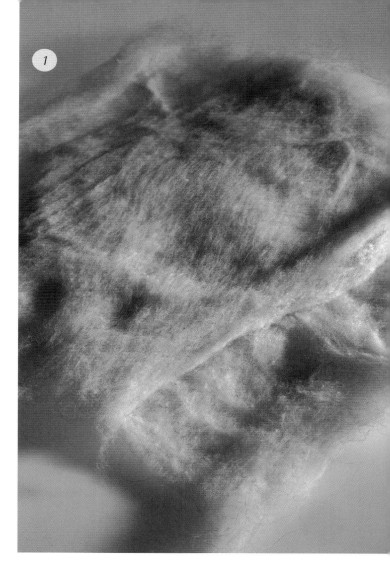

Place 4 layers over each other with the fibres of the first layer lying vertically, the fibres of the second layer vertically, the fibres of the third layer horizontally (at a 90° angle to the first two layers), and the last layer vertically again. Press down the layers lightly to make it easier to roll them up (see figure 1).

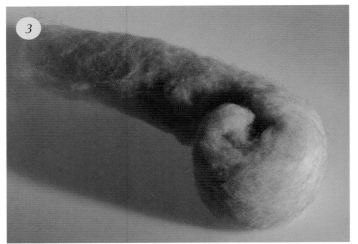

Place the wool layers in front of you on the table and roll them up into a firm roll. The tighter the roll is wound, the quicker it is to needle-felt (see figure 2).

Now roll up this long roll like a snail shell (see figure 3). Again, the tighter the better. Do not roll it right up to the end, but leave an opening for Thumbling

Place the rolled-up snail shell on the felting mat and compress the fibres by repeatedly stick-ing the felting needle in and out of it. Once suffi-ciently compressed, emphasise the spiral coils of the shell by repeatedly poking the needle in and out along the grooves of the coil (see figure 4).

Make the opening for Thumbling by stick-ing the needle in and out of the wide, not quite rolled up end. If you cannot make the opening deep enough to hold Thumbling using the felting needle, carefully cut out some wool and then continue needle-felting the opening into shape.

The snail shell looks particularly pretty if you needle-felt some thin layers of a different colour of wool over the surface of the shell. You can also needle-felt a thin strand of different coloured sheep's wool along the shell's spiral coils for emphasis.

Thumbling

Make the doll according to the basic pattern. The exact measurements are given on p.23.

Cut Thumbling's suit out of green felt. First sew the outer seams, then the inner leg seams. Turn it right side out and smooth the seams.

Put the suit on Thumbling and run a gathering thread around the neck opening. Fold any excess leg length upwards. Wind a piece of wool yarn around the doll's waist for a belt.

Cut the hat out of brown felt, sew it together and turn right side out. Needle-felt the magic wool hair to the head and cut into it to make a shaggy edge. Position the hat on the head with the seam at the front and fasten it tight with a few stitches or craft glue.

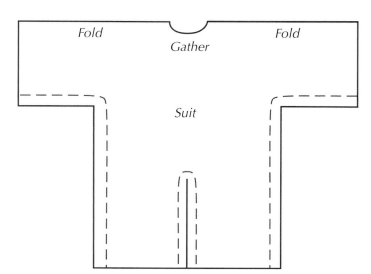

Fold   *Fold*
Gather
Suit

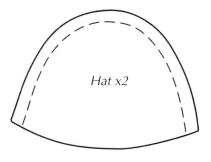

Hat x2

Rumpelstiltskin

Transparencies are a completely different way of depicting a fairy tale. They impart a cosy atmosphere, particularly during the evenings of early autumn. The flickering candlelight behind the transparency causes different colour impressions and has a calming effect on the observer. They are also simple to make and are suitable for a birthday present.

Although you could make a transparency based on any of the fairy tales in this book, I chose Rumpelstiltskin because the atmosphere of this fairy tale scene is represented wonderfully by this medium: Rumpelstiltskin dancing around his fire in the woods, not realizing that he is being overheard.

Materials

Black construction (sugar) paper for the frame
Black drawing paper for the figure and the house
White, yellow, orange, red, light green, dark
   green and blue tissue paper
Glue stick
Gold star stickers
Sharp scissors

Draw the frame on to the black construction paper and cut it out with a sharp pair of scissors.

Cut the house, Rumpelstiltskin, the messenger and the firewood out of black drawing paper.

Fold back the two side parts of the frame as shown in the pattern. If necessary, score the fold lines with a knife first, using a ruler.

Glue white tissue paper behind the middle and side parts of the frame with a glue stick. Glue all further bits on to this background. Glue red tissue paper behind the roof slit and yellow behind the door and window of the house. Now cut out the different bits of fire and glue them to the large yellow circle in the shape of a fire.

It's now best to work with the transparency placed on a light box or carefully stuck to the window.

Glue Rumpelstiltskin to the transparency and then the fire with the firewood behind him. Glue the first layer of grass to the lower edge of the transparency picture. Then glue the second layer on, with the blades of grass interspersed. Now glue the house and the messenger to the two side parts.

Cut out the meadow as you please. It has three layers. Glue the meadow to the lower edge first and then very lightly trace the outlines of the yellow fire circle on to it with a pencil. Then cut this bit out of the meadow so that the fire remains yellow and bright and is not covered. Glue the meadow around the yellow circle. Glue the meadow behind the house and windows in the same way so that the yellow is not covered by the meadow.

Draw a moon into the centre of the generously pre-cut sky and cut it out. Again, first glue the sky only to the upper edge. Then trace the outlines of the meadow and the fire and cut the blue sky accordingly. Glue the sky all around. Glue gold stars to the back of the sky.

Cut out the fir trees and spread them around as you please at the edge of the meadow. The more they overlap, the more they appear like a real forest. Make the trees on the side section in the same way.

To finish, glue a sheet of white tissue paper behind the whole picture and cut off the edges cleanly.

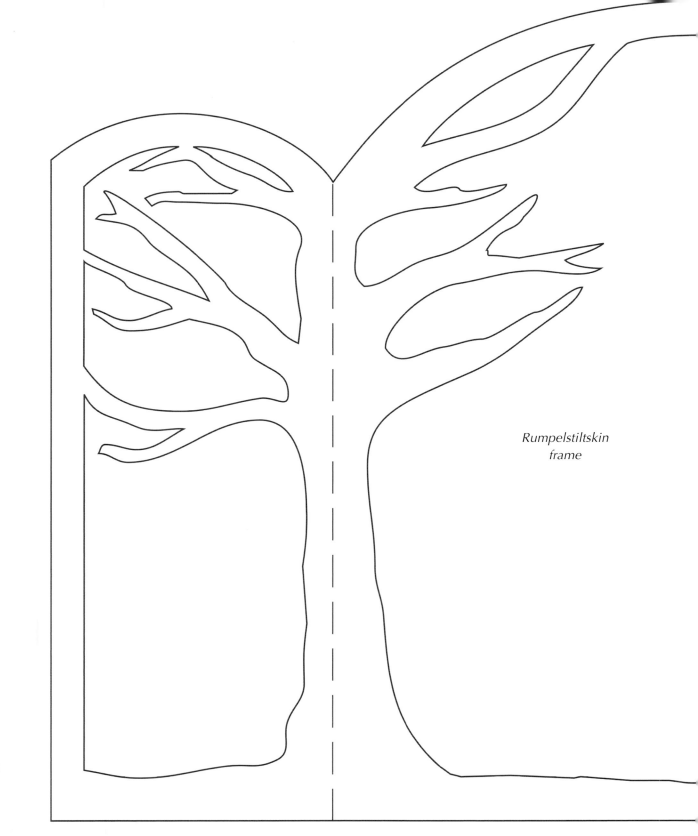

Rumpelstiltskin frame

52

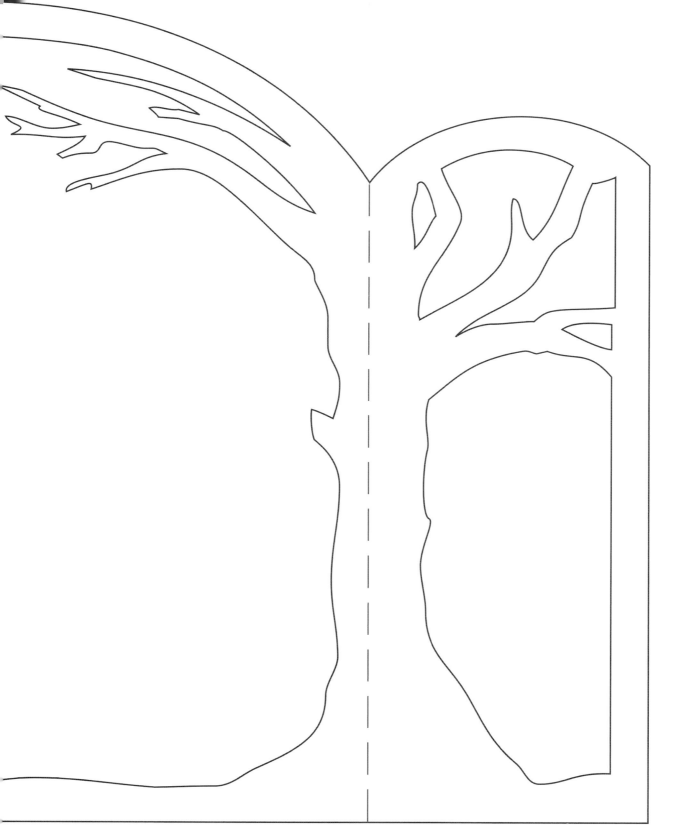

Grass
Light green tissue paper

x2 for all three sides

Dark green tissue paper
Cut further layers as you please

Messenger x1

Rumpelstiltskin x1

House x1

Fir trees

Green tissue paper

55

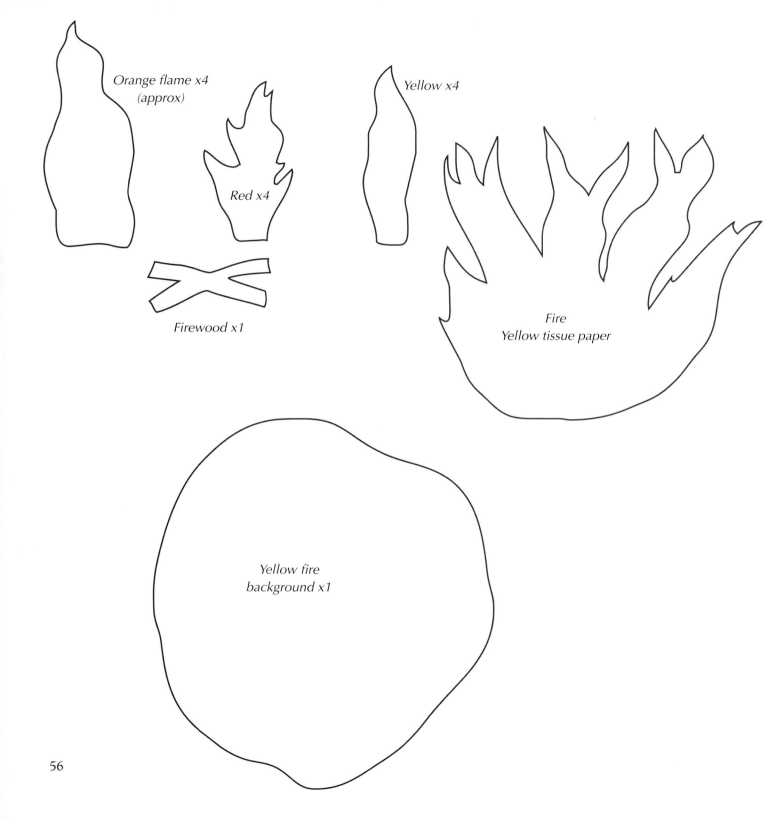

Orange flame x4
(approx)

Red x4

Yellow x4

Firewood x1

Fire
Yellow tissue paper

Yellow fire
background x1

Brother and Sister

The time of year is not quite clear in the Brother and Sister fairy tale, but as hunting is usually an autumn sport, it seems to fit best here.

For this fairy tale I used the wooden board from Hansel and Gretel and the house from Snow White to show you how the props can be used in different ways.

You can drill holes into the wooden base as you please, and push real twigs into the holes to make the trees. This gives this fairy tale setting a completely different look, but is very simple to do.

The prince is the same doll as used for Sleeping Beauty, see p.37 for full instructions. You can easily change the scene in this setting, too. First you can just having the sister and her brother the deer, and then add the prince towards the end of the fairy tale period.

This scene looks particularly effective with a tea light or a small salt lamp behind it, so that the trees cast shadows.

Materials
Purple silk for the dress
Some hand-felted grey felt (or craft felt) for the cape
Purple felt for the top
White felt for the underpants
Curly wool fur for the hair
Brown sheep's wool for the shoes
Small beads for the hem of the dress
Toy deer (this one is by Ostheimer)
Gold thread or braid for the deer's collar

Sister doll
Make the doll according to the instructions given in the basic patterns. For exact measurements, see p.23.

DRESS

Use the pattern given for Sleeping Beauty, p.37. If the dress is too long at the hem, shorten it slightly and hem it up. You can sew small pink beads to the hem if you please.

Do not gather the dress under the arms with a velvet band, rather let it fall down loosely. The velvet ribbon at the hem should also be left out.

Instead, the sister has a purple bodice. Cut the top following the pattern. Put it on the doll and sew the back seam. Sew the sides of the bodice under the arms with 2–3 stitches.

UNDERPANTS

Use the pattern and instructions given for Sleeping Beauty.

SHOES

To make the shoes, wind brown magic wool around the sister's feet and then felt them on lightly.

CAPE

Cut the cape out of the grey felt following the pattern and put it over the doll's shoulders. If necessary, sew it together under the arms with 2–3 stitches.

HAIR

Make the sister's hair out of curly wool fur. Cut it out following the wig pattern given in Snow White and Rose Red.

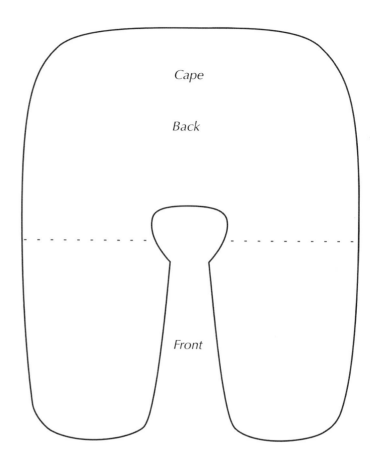

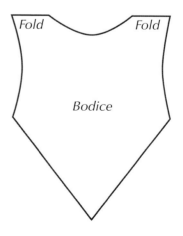

Winter

Snow White and the Seven Dwarfs

The scene for Snow White and the Seven Dwarfs is more elaborate. You can make it bit by bit.

The gnome's house was made together with the children. First we gathered bits of bark and lichen, and then we sawed, sanded and glued the house together. As a base for the scene I used a large baking tray, which allowed plenty of space for the house, the trees and the surroundings. We laid a large felted sheet over it and then needle-felted the flowers etc. on to it.

At the end of autumn children are particularly aware of gnomes as they are often seen displayed in schools and nurseries or at the lantern walk in Waldorf schools. And so this fairy tale is particularly suited to this time of year.

The gnomes in this fairy tale work in mines under the earth mining crystals. The scene shows the gnomes coming home to Snow White after work with a cart full of crystals. Naturally the gnomes can also appear one after the other out of

the woods, so that you don't have to make them all at once.

In this setting I have used a different way of lighting the scene: a chain of fairy lights, which is fastened to the baking tray underneath the meadow felt. The small mushroom heads are made from real Chinese lantern flowers.

Materials

SNOW WHITE
White cotton for the blouse and underpants
White broderie anglaise or white lace for the
   skirt 23 x 8 cm (9 x 3 ¼ in)
Red felt for the jacket
Black magic wool for the hair

GNOMES
Coloured magic wool
Skin-coloured wool batting
Pipe cleaners
Curly wool for the hair and beards

HOUSE
Plywood, 4 mm (¹/₈ in) thick
Bark, lichens or moss
Hot glue gun

TREES
Styrofoam cones
Different shades of green magic wool

MUSHROOM LIGHTS
A green fairy-light chain with 10 bulbs
White masking tape
5 large dried Chinese lantern flowers

Snow White
Make the doll according to the instructions given in the basic pattern. The exact measurements can be found on p.23.

BLOUSE
Cut the blouse out of white cotton fabric. Sew the side and sleeve seams and cut into the fabric under the arms 3–4 times to stop the seam

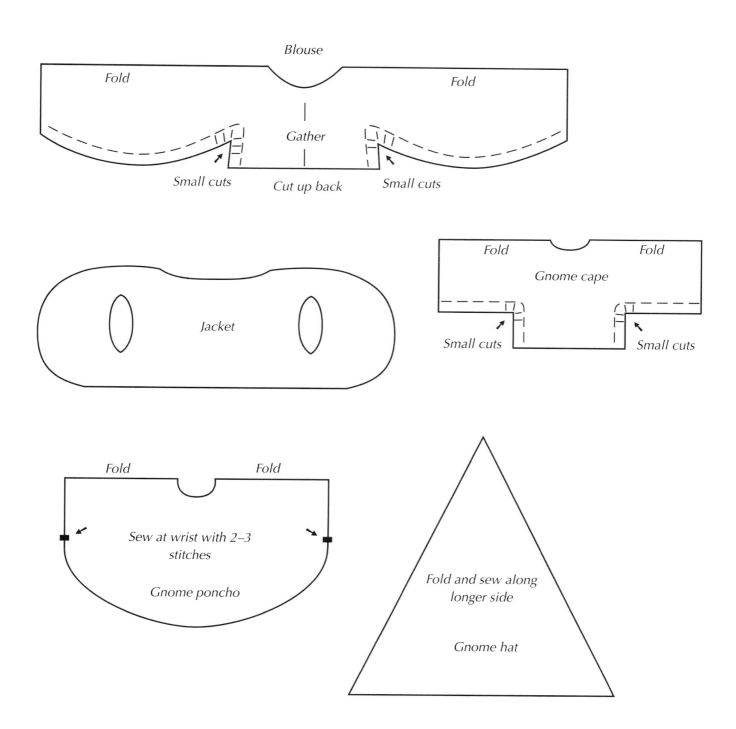

Blouse

Fold

Fold

Gather

Small cuts

Cut up back

Small cuts

Jacket

Fold

Fold

Gnome cape

Small cuts

Small cuts

Fold

Fold

Sew at wrist with 2–3 stitches

Gnome poncho

Fold and sew along longer side

Gnome hat

puckering. Turn the blouse right side out and smooth the seams well.

Now put the blouse on your doll and sew the back seam. If necessary, run a gathering thread around the neck opening. Fold the fabric at the wrists and run a gathering thread around to hem it, then pull the thread tight.

SKIRT

Make the skirt out of broderie anglaise or lace, 23 x 8 cm (9 x 3 ¼ in). Sew the back seam. Fold the top edge and run a gathering thread around to hem it.

Put the skirt on the doll and pull the gathering thread to the desired width. Sew the skirt to the blouse with mattress stitch.

JACKET

Cut the jacket out of red felt. Put the jacket on your doll and sew the front seam shut with two cross stitches.

Gnomes

You can give each gnome a completely different look: some large, some small, some fat, some thin. You can also vary the hat and coat colours and styles.

HEAD AND BODY

Pull an approximately 15 cm (6 in) long strand out of the skin-coloured wool batting. Make a knot in the centre for the head. Then spread the wool still hanging out the knot around the knot. The head should now be approximately 5 cm (2 in) circumference.

Tie a thread directly below the head around the hanging down sheep's wool. This wool is used later to make the gnome's body. Divide the wool hanging out under the head into two strands and place a 9 cm (3 1/2 in) long pipe cleaner between the strands for the arms. Tie off the sheep's wool again under the arms to hold the pipe cleaner in place.

Fold the wool remaining below the arms in half and needle-felt in place. You can vary the size of the gnome by not folding it exactly in half.

Wind wool around the arms as described for the other dolls, p.18. Adjust the length of the arm pipe cleaners to suit the size of the gnome.

Needle-felt the body from all sides to make a single column of wool. Mark the legs by firmly needle-felting along a line along the centre of the column. Cut the legs apart along the needle-felted groove and needle-felt them slightly round (See above).

To make the gnome's clothes, tightly wind magic wool around the body, arms and legs, using the colour and thickness you want. Needle-felt the clothes in place. Needle-felt the end of the legs, where the shoes will be added.

There are now different ways of proceeding: the red gnome was made using only needle-felting. Red braces were also needle-felted to the body. The hat is made out of homemade felt (see instructions, p.19). This gnome was also used for Snow White and Rose Red. The other gnomes have coats or capes made out of craft felt.

SHOES

To make the shoes, fold over a small strand of wool and needle-felt it into a shoe shape. Needle-felt the back more firmly and the front more loosely. This makes the shape of a shoe, which is flat at the heel and higher at the front. Attach the shoes to the legs by needle-felting them to the end of the legs.

FACE, BEARD AND HAIR

Make the face using the same techniques as the other dolls (see p.14). You probably will not need to make a mouth as the beard is usually needle-felted over the mouth area.

Needle-felt beard and hair to the head using curly wool.

Setting

HOUSE

The gnome's house is a very basic plywood construction. Saw two rectangles, 15.5 x 18.5 cm (6 1/8 x 7 1/4 in), for the roof. To make the front and back walls, saw two triangles with a 20 cm (8 in) base and 18.5 cm (7 1/4 in) side lengths. Saw a doorway into the front triangle.

Glue the parts together with a hot glue gun. I pushed the front and back walls inwards slightly to make the roof jut out over the vertical walls.

Glue bark to the roof with a hot glue gun, adding lichens or moss to the bare spaces between the bark.

TREES

Styrofoam cones can be purchased in a variety of sizes to make different sized trees.

Needle-felt a basic colour around the entire cone. Needle-felt different lengths and thicknesses of wool strands to make branches. It is best to start at the base and gradually work upwards to the tip of the tree.

Wind white masking tape just below the bulbs of 2 fairy lights to group them in twos, the tape makes the stalk of the mushroom.

Cut crosses into the green felt sheet at the points where you want the mushrooms to stand. Push the taped together lamps through the felt. Fasten the fairy-light wires to the baking tray with masking tape, and place the green felt meadow over them. Straighten the lamps.

Cut small slits into the bottom of dried Chinese lantern flowers and push them over the lights. The lights never get hot enough to set the dried flowers on fire.

ACCESSORIES

The small accessories used in the scene, such as the lantern and cart can be purchased from a well-stocked craft shop.

Hansel and Gretel

This fairy tale setting is quite complicated to make. For a base, we cut and sanded the wooden board to size and then drilled holes for the fence. We made the fence, which is described in further detail below. Then we gathered moss for the base and small stones for the path.

The fir tree method explained for this scene shows you how to make a 'quicker' kind of tree, but you can make any of the trees described in the other fairy tale settings if you prefer.

Once you have finished the landscape, you can use it for the first fairy tale evening with Hansel and Gretel, who walk alone through forests and meadows, lit only by candlelight.

In our family the witch was always awaited with great excitement. But first we had to bake and decorate the witch's house. We did this before advent, and then the children were allowed to eat the witch's house when we stopped reading the fairy tale on December 6th. We would have a small celebration with friends. Just as Hansel and Gretel found many treasures, each child found a small crystal inside the house that they were allowed to keep.

Materials

HANSEL

Blue craft felt for the jacket
Blue felt for the trousers
Brown craft felt for the sandals
Strong cardboard for the sandals
Light coloured cotton fabric for the shirt
3 small glass beads for the jacket buttons
Contrasting thread for the trouser patches
Dark brown fake fur for the hair
Small sponge for the gingerbread

GRETEL

Orange craft felt for the dress
Grey homemade felt for the jacket
Contrasting thread for the trouser patches
Brown craft felt for the shoes
1 cm (3/8 in) wide elastic band for the under-
    pants
Blond long-haired fake fur for the hair

WITCH

Dark brown craft felt for the skirt
Small remnants of fabric for the patches

Cotton fabric for the blouse and the headscarf
Black wool yarn for the triangular shawl
Grey magic wool for the hair and the eyebrows
2 cm (3/4 in) wide elastic band for the underpants

SETTING

Brown construction (sugar) paper
Wooden skewer for the shovel

Hansel

Make the doll according to the instructions given in the basic patterns. For exact measurements, see p.23.

SHIRT

Cut the shirt out of light-coloured cotton fabric. Sew the side and arm seams. Now cut into the excess fabric at the armpit nearly up to the seam a few times to stop the seam puckering. Turn the shirt right side out and iron it. Put the shirt on the doll.

Now sew the back seam by folding over one edge and placing it over the other loose edge. Pin it in place and sew the seam with mattress stitch.

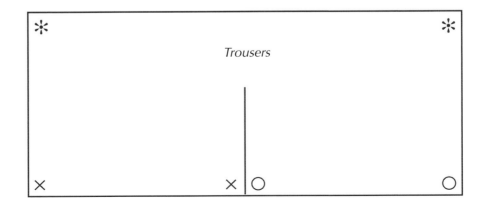

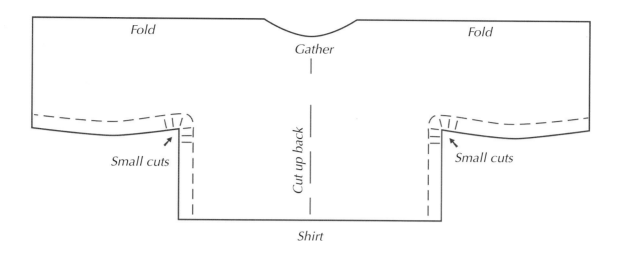

Fold   Gather   Fold

Small cuts   Cut up back   Small cuts

Shirt

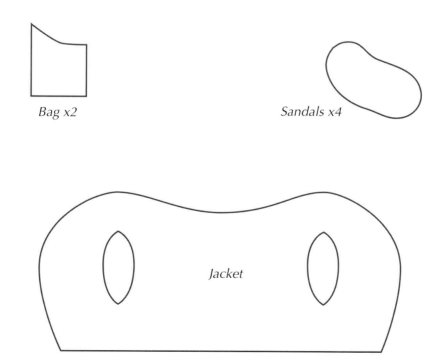

Bag x2

Sandals x4

Jacket

excess fabric at the front one side over the other to make the fly. Sew it together with mattress stitch.

To finish, sew patches on to the trousers by sewing three large stitches closely together, with two stitches on top of them. Fold the trousers legs up if desired.

SANDALS

Cut the sandal sole pattern out of brown felt 4 times, and out of strong cardboard twice. Glue the felt soles to the top and bottom of the cardboard soles using craft glue and let them dry well.

Cut the straps to fit the size of the foot, strap width approximately 0.3 cm (1/8 in). Sew the straps to the right and left of the sole with a few stitches. Remember to make a left and a right shoe. Glue the sandals to the doll's feet.

JACKET

Cut the jacket out of blue craft felt. Sew blanket stitches around the jacket edge and the armholes. Sew on the 3 small glass beads as buttons.

HAIR

Cut the hair out of fake fur. Proceed as described on p.16.

GINGER BREAD

Hansel and Gretel each have a piece of gingerbread in their hand from nibbling at the house. To make the gingerbread, put a small tuft of brown sheep's wool on to a sponge, fold it over and poke the felting needle in and out until the gingerbread is the desired shape (square or heart). If necessary you can draw the outline of the gingerbread to the sponge as a pattern.

To finish, needle-felt almonds on to the gingerbread using white wool.

Fold back the sleeves as necessary, then run a gathering thread around the wrists and pull it tight. Sew the thread ends in well and cut them off.

TROUSERS

Cut the trousers out of blue felt. Fold the trousers as shown in the pattern and sew the seams, starting with the legs. Sew the back seam last. Turn the trousers right side out and iron well.

Put the trousers on the doll and arrange the

Gretel

Make the doll according to the instructions in the basic patterns. For exact measurements see p.23.

DRESS

Cut the dress top out of the orange craft felt without seam allowance. Test the length on the actual size of your doll. Sew the side and sleeve seams with backstitch. Turn the dress right side out and put it on your doll. Sew the back seam with a few small stitches.

Now cut a rectangle 14 x 6.5 cm (5 1/2 x 2 1/2 in) out of orange craft felt to make the skirt of the dress. Sew the back seam and turn the skirt right side out. Run a gathering thread around the top edge. Now put the skirt on your doll.

Sew the skirt to the top with mattress stitch. Gather the thread to the desired length and sew it in well. To finish, sew patches on to the dress.

JACKET

Cut the jacket out of homemade felt. Put the jacket over the shoulders of the doll and sew it under the arms with 2–3 stitches.

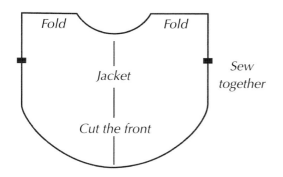

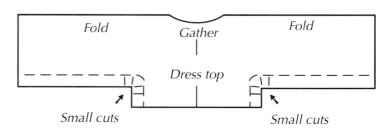

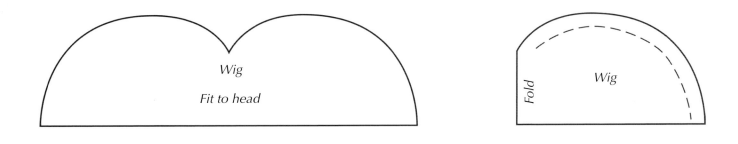

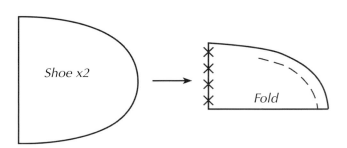

SHOES

Cut 2 sets of the shoe pattern out of brown craft felt. Sew the front seam shown in the pattern with backstitch and turn the shoe right side out. Try it on the foot. If necessary stretch the shoe with a blunt lead pencil. Sew the back seam with blanket stitches.

UNDERPANTS

Cut a 6 cm (2 3/8 in) length of the elastic band, and sew the ends together with a few back-stitches. With the seam is at the centre of the back, sew 2 stitches to the centre of the bottom edge of the elastic band, between the legs. Put the underpants on the doll.

HAIR

Cut the hair out of the blond piece of fake fur, following the pattern provided. Proceed as described on p.16.

Witch

Make the doll according to the basic pattern. For exact measurements, see p.23.

To make the witch's hunchback, needle-felt a bit of wool to the back between the shoulders.

Make the nose larger by needle-felting some more sheep's wool on to it. There is also a wart on the nose. You can make it by drawing it on with a slightly wetted tip of a black pencil or by needle-felting on 2–3 threads of black sheep's wool.

Make the chin pointy by needle-felting it (see p.12).

Needle-felt the eyebrows using grey sheep's wool.

BLOUSE

Cut the blouse out of thin cotton fabric without seam allowance. Sew the side and sleeve seams. Cut into the excess fabric under the arms 4–5 times, nearly up to the seam, to stop the seam puckering. Turn the blouse right side out and iron it well. Put the blouse on your doll.

Now sew the back seam by folding over one edge and placing it over the other loose edge of fabric. Pin it in place and sew it together with mattress stitch.

Fray the sleeve edgings slightly. If necessary, fold the neck opening inwards and sew it in place with a running seam.

UNDERPANTS

Cut an 8 cm (3 1/8 in) length of elastic band. Now make it in the same way as described for Gretel.

SKIRTS

The witch is wearing two skirts on top of each other. Re-measure the exact length on your doll.

Cut 2 rectangles out of brown craft felt. Make

one rectangle 19 cm (7 1/2 in) long and 9.5 cm (3 3/4 in) high, and the other 19 cm (7 1/2 in) long and 7.5 cm (3 in) high. Hem the higher rectangle by 1 cm (3/8 in) to give it more stability.

Now sew the back seams of both skirts with backstitch.

Glue a few patches randomly on to the shorter (top) skirt with craft glue.

Put both skirts together. Make sure the short

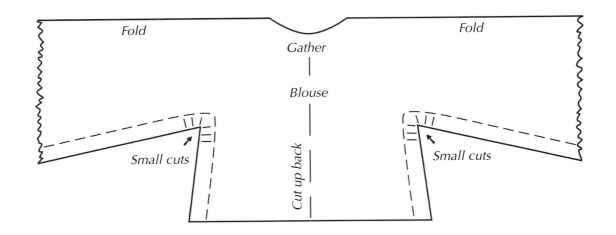

Fold   Gather   *Fold*

Blouse

Cut up back

Small cuts   *Small cuts*

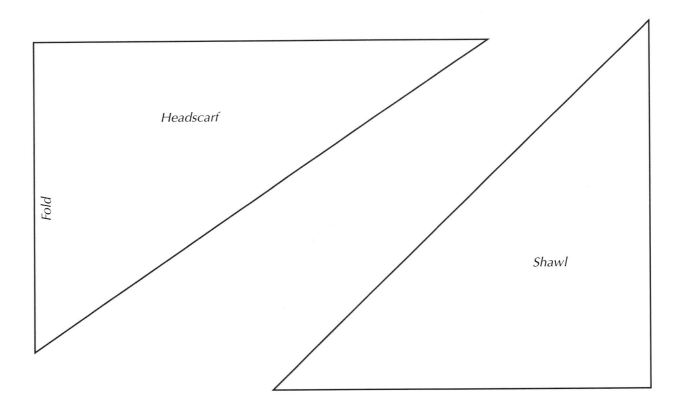

Headscarf

Fold

Shawl

skirt with the patches is on top. Run a gathering thread around the top edge of both skirts. Put the skirts on the doll, pull the gathering thread to the desired length and sew the threads in well.

HAIR AND HEADSCARF

Needle-felt grey sheep's wool around the head for the hair.

Cut the scarf out of cotton fabric. Try it on the head and if necessary make it smaller. Do not hem it.

TRIANGULAR SHAWL

Crochet the shawl out of black wool yarn. As each kind of wool has a different tension, crochet the shawl to fit the pattern size.

Knot the fringe to the two shorter sides of the shawl.

Put the shawl on the witch and sew it together at the front with 2–3 stitches.

Put a twig in the witch's hand for a walking stick.

Setting

BASE

I used a wooden board from a DIY store as a base, 40 x 30 cm (15 $^3/_4$ x 11 $^3/_4$ in).

Round off the corners of the board and round the edges slightly.

Drill small holes along the front edge of the board, approximately 2 cm ($^3/_4$ in) apart, for the fence. Stick small twigs into these holes to make the poles of the fence. Soak some longer twigs in water to soften them, then weave them around the fence poles.

Make the path with small pebbles; cover the rest of the base in moss.

OVEN

Cut the four parts of the oven out of brown construction paper. Cut small slits into the top curve of the front and back sides as shown in the pattern. This makes it easier to fold back the arch. Bend back the edges along the dotted line. Cut the flap door out of the front section and bend the straight edge outwards along the dotted line.

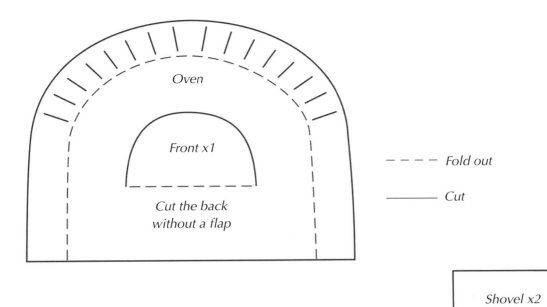

Oven

Front x1

Cut the back
without a flap

- - - - Fold out

───── Cut

Shovel x2

Central section x1

SHOVEL

Cut the two parts of the shovel out of brown construction paper. Shorten the wooden skewer to the length desired. Glue the skewer to the centre of one of the shovel halves and then glue the other half against it.

GINGERBREAD HOUSE

500 g (1 lb) honey
500 g (1 lb) flour
125 g (4 1/2 oz) butter
5 eggs
1 1/2 teaspoons cocoa
1 1/2 teaspoons cinnamon
1 pinch of ground cloves
1 packet of baking powder

Warm the honey and the butter together until the butter has melted. Make sure it doesn't boil.

Now add all the other ingredients and mix.

Roll out the finished dough in two baking trays and bake in the oven at 220°C (430°F) for 15 minutes.

Cut the finished gingerbread slabs while still warm.

For the roof, cut out two rectangles 21 x 20.5 cm (8 1/4 x 8 in). For the front and back walls cut out two triangles, the base 18.5 cm (7 1/4 cm) and the sides 23.5 cm (9 1/4 in) long.

To stick the parts together, use a paste made with 2 egg whites beaten stiff and 400 g (14 oz) icing sugar. Use this paste to stick sweets, nuts and biscuits to the house for decoration.

Mother Holle

The setting of Mother Holle shows yet another way of depicting fairy tale scenes. As Mother Holle is more of an airy being, she is the natural choice for a suspended fairy tale scene. I decided to use a birch branch wreath, which makes the flying feathers and falling snow look very impressive. You could also suspend her from a branch and hang the feathers and snowflakes around her to make a mobile. If you do suspend her directly from a branch, make sure you attach the thread to her hat or the back of her dress, rather than around her neck, as this may upset children.

Materials

MOTHER HOLLE

Light blue craft felt
Dark blue craft felt
White cotton fabric for the blouse and pillow
Broderie anglaise for the petticoat
4 cm (1 1/2 in) wide lace for the bonnet
1 cm (3/8 in) wide lace for the collar
2 small white beads for buttons
white sheep's wool for the hair.

BIRCH WREATH

Birch branches
Wire
White sheep's wool
Thread
White feathers
Strong thread or ribbon for suspending

Mother Holle

Make the doll according to the instructions given in the basic pattern. You will find the exact measurements on p.23.

Needle-felt the hair to the head using white sheep's wool.

Blouse

Cut the blouse out of white cotton fabric. Sew the side and sleeve seams and cut into the fabric under the arms 3–4 times to stop the seam puckering. Turn the blouse right side out and if necessary iron the seams well.

Put the blouse on the doll and sew the front seam with mattress stitch. Run a gathering thread around the neck opening. Pull it together to the desired width. Do the same with the sleeve endings.

To make the collar, cut a piece of the 1 cm (3/8 in) wide lace, run a gathering thread around the edge and place it around the neck of the doll. Sew the collar closed at the front with 2–3 stitches.

To finish, sew 2–3 beads as buttons to the front of the blouse.

Petticoat

Cut a rectangle out of the broderie anglaise, 20 x 7.5 cm (8 x 3 in). Sew the back seam. Narrowly fold over the upper edge and run a gathering thread along it. Put the petticoat on your doll up to the arms. Pull the gathering thread to the desired width.

Skirt

Cut a rectangle out of light blue craft felt, 17 x 7 cm (6 3/4 x 2 3/4 in). Make the skirt in the same way as the petticoat.

Apron

Cut the apron out of light blue craft felt, using the pattern. Fold the apron strings in half lengthwise and tie the apron on the doll.

Bonnet

Cut a 12 cm (4 3/4 in) long piece of the 4 cm (1 1/2 in) wide lace for the bonnet. Fold the lace in half lengthwise (4 x 6 cm) and run a gathering thread along the longer edge. Pull the thread until the edge is 2 cm (3/4 in) wide and sew in the ends. This is the back of the bonnet.

Run a further gathering thread around the bonnet approximately 1 cm (3/8 in) away from the edge. Now put the bonnet on the doll and pull the front gathering thread to the desired length. Sew the bonnet tight to the right and left of the head.

PILLOW

Cut a rectangle of white cotton fabric, 8 x 5 cm (3 1/8 in x 2 in). Fold it in half, wrong sides together, and sew two sides completely and half of one side shut.

Turn the pillow right side out through the remaining opening and stuff it lightly.

Sew the pillowcase to Mother Holle's hands.

Birch wreath

Cut a few birch branches (without leaves) for the birch wreath and twist them together lightly. Wind a strong wire around the lower section to hold the branches together.

Thread several sheep's wool balls on to threads. Fasten theses snowflake strings to the reverse upper part of the wreath so they hang down.

Cover the wire at the bottom with white sheep's wool to look like snow.

To finish, spread feathers out around the wreath and glue them in place. They add a lot of life as they move with every draft.

Glue Mother Holle to the snow and feathers with a hot glue gun.

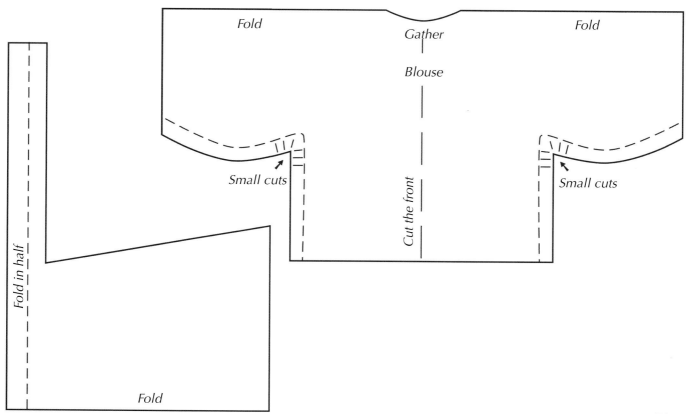

Additional Tales and Scenes

Star Money

The Star Money fairy tale was our special birthday fairy tale, as described in the chapter, Using Fairy Tale Scenes with Children, p.9.

The base is a round wooden board, for example, a chopping board, covered with moss. The surrounding is made up of a small rock crystals, mushrooms and fir trees. Any more would detract from the glittering star rain falling into Star Money's lap.

The scene looks especially beautiful if you place several tea lights behind Star Money so they shine through the sky.

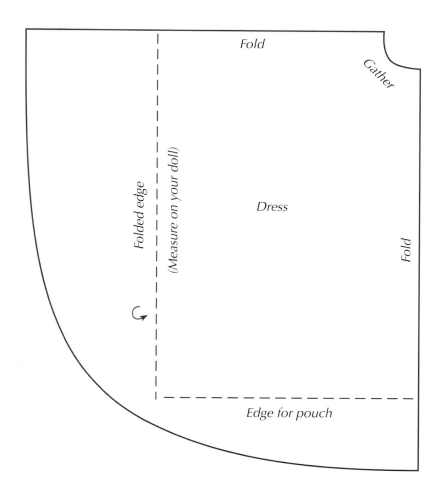

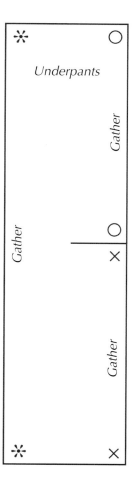

Materials

STAR MONEY DOLL
White silk
Light yellow unspun silk strand or fur remnant
   for the hair
White felt for the underpants
Small gold stars with a hole
Small gold stars without a hole
Blue sewing thread

SETTING
Large balloon approximately 100 cm (40 in) cir-
   cumference
Wallpaper paste
Tissue paper: medium blue, light green and dark
   green
Small gold star stickers
Gold stars with a hole for sewing on

Star Money
Make the head and body as described in the basic
patterns. You will find the exact measurements on
p.23.

UNDERPANTS
Cut a rectangle out of white felt following the
pattern. Fold the rectangle in half as shown in
the pattern (star to star, circle to circle etc.). Cut
into the centre of the bottom edge as shown in
the pattern. First sew the back seam with small
blanket stitches, then the leg seams with small
backstitches. Turn the underpants right side out
and smooth the seams well.

Run a gathering thread along the top and leg
edges. Then put the trousers on the doll, push the
trouser legs up, pull the gathering threads tight
and sew in the ends.

DRESS
The dress is sewn directly on the doll. Cut the
dress out of white silk without seam allowance.
Put the dress on the doll. Then sew the dress
seams with a few stitches as described below.

Fold back the neck edge and run a gathering
thread around it. Measure the distance between
the neck and the wrist. Fold back the excess fabric at the wrists. The fabric should fall loosely and
not be taut at all. Sew the fabric under the wrists
with 2–3 stitches.

To make a small pouch for catching the gold
stars, fold back the dress approximately 2 cm
(3/4 in) from the bottom edge and run a gathering
thread along this fold from right to left. Then pull
the thread slightly and sew the right end to the
right wrist, and the left end to the left wrist.

HAIR
Use yellow unspun silk or a fur remnant for the
hair. Sew the hair to head with lots of small
stitches (see p.16 for further instructions). Glue
the stars without a hole around the head like a
crown.

Setting

BACKDROP/SKY
Blow the balloon up until it is approximately
100 cm (40 in) circumference. Rip the blue tissue paper into small strips. Glue the strips to the
balloon as shown. To do this, coat the balloon bit
by bit with wallpaper paste, place the strips of
tissue paper on to it and apply more wallpaper
paste. The pieces of paper should overlap. Cover
the balloon in this way with at least 3–4 layers of
tissue paper.

To make a lighter triangle at the centre of the sky (for the star rain), apply only two layers of unripped transparency paper to that part.

Place the side of the balloon that hasn't been covered in paper into a pot and leave it to dry well. When the glue has dried and hardened, separate the tissue paper from the balloon by pricking and bursting the balloon, leaving your Star Money sky intact.

Hold the transparency up to the light. If you are not happy with the way it looks, you can add further layers of tissue paper to any part. Now cut the edges of the sky straight and the front edge straight or wavy.

Take a blue thread and knot it around one of the stars with a hole, then thread another star a little further down the thread and knot it in place. Repeat this until the star thread is as long as you want. Make at least 4 star threads.

Thread the end of the star thread into a small sharp needle and push the needle through the top of your sky scene. Knot the thread well. Suspend the remaining star threads in the same way to make it look as if the stars are falling from the sky.

Stick gold star stickers to the back of the sky scene.

Front

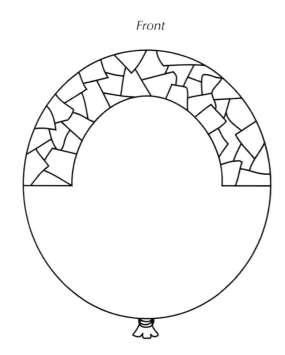

Back

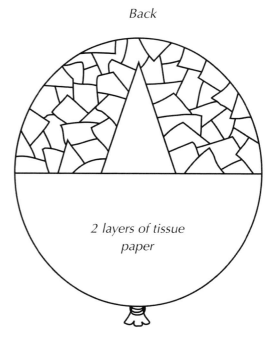

2 layers of tissue paper

FIR TREES

You will need 8 layers of green tissue paper for each fir tree. Cut 8 rectangles following the pattern measurements. Fold the top sheet in half lengthwise and unfold again. Sew all the 8 layers together along this fold. You can either use a sewing machine or sew the seam by hand.

Place the centre of the tree pattern over this seam and draw around the outline with a lead pencil. Cut the eight-layered fir tree out.

To finish, fan out the layers to make the fir tree three-dimensional.

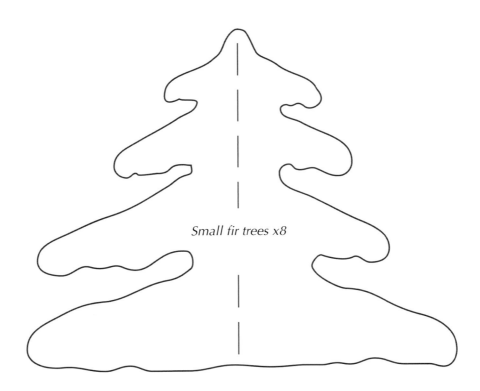

Small fir trees x8

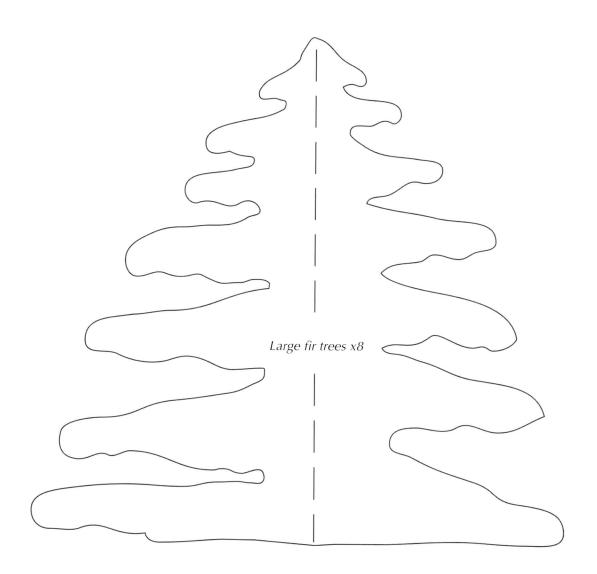

Large fir trees x8

The Royal Family

The full royal family is not shown in any of the fairy tale scenes in this book and also not specifically assigned to any fairy tale. This section shows how to make a king, queen, princess and castle turret, which you will be able to use for any scenes you may choose from other fairy tales.

Materials

KING
Dark red felt for the robe
Dark red velveteen for the cloak
Gold braid for the belt
Gold braid for the crown
Curly wool for the hair
White sheep's wool for the cape edging
Black felt tip pen
Wooden skewers
Wooden bead
Gold paint
Craft glue

QUEEN
Pink craft felt for the underdress
Dark red velveteen for the dress and cloak
Gold braid for the belt and sleeves
Gold braid for the crown
Gold beads for the necklace
Long-haired blond fake fur for the hair

PRINCESS
White felt for the blouse
White felt with gold dots for the dress (or suitable alternative)
2 small gold beads for buttons
Thin gold braid for the dress and headband
Strand of unspun silk for the hair

CASTLE TURRET
Grey felt for the castle turret, 45 cm (17 3/4 in) wide, 30 cm (11 3/4 in) high
Green felt for ivy
2 beads for the entrance gate
Grey felt tip pen

King

Make the doll according to the instructions given in the basic patterns. Exact measurements are given on p.23. The only difference is the arm length, which is 14 cm (5 $\frac{1}{2}$ in) plus 1 cm ($\frac{3}{8}$ in) extra for folding over each side.

ROBE

Cut the king's robe out of dark red felt without seam allowance. Sew the left and right side seams. Turn the robe right side out and smooth the seams well.

Put the robe on the doll and run a gathering thread around the neck opening. Run a gathering thread 1 cm ($\frac{3}{8}$ in) away from each sleeve ending and pull tight.

Wind a gold braid around the king's waist for a belt. Tie a knot at each end to stop the braid unravelling.

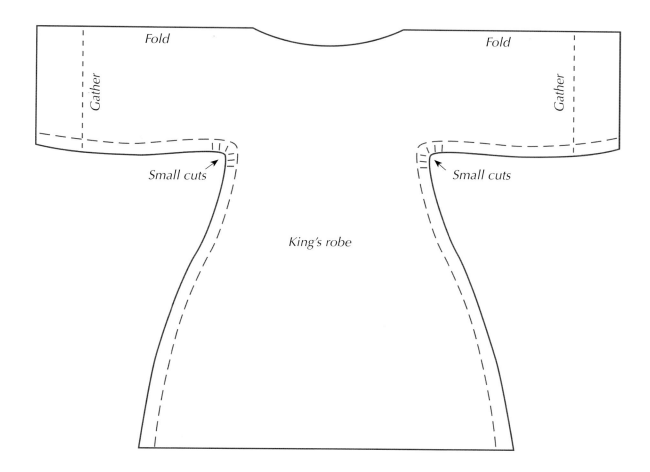

Fold

Gather

Fold

Gather

Small cuts

Small cuts

King's robe

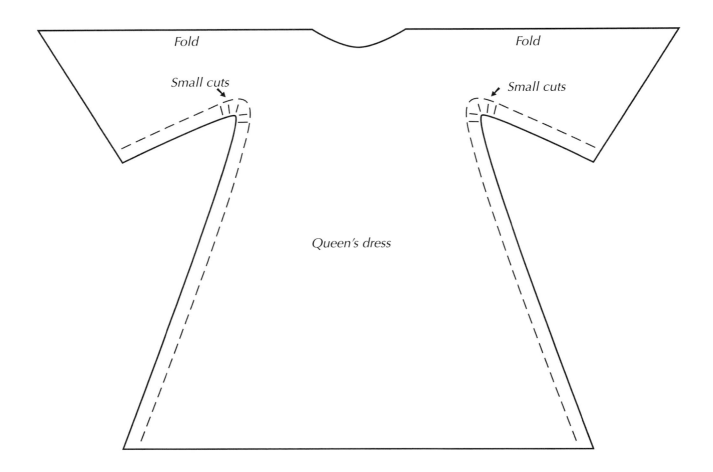

Fold

Fold

Small cuts

Small cuts

Queen's dress

CLOAK

Cut a square, 16 x 16 cm (6 ¼ x 6 ¼ in) out of the velveteen. Round off the bottom corners slightly. Take a piece of white wool batting to fit around the bottom and two sides of the cloak. Twist the strand between your hands to make it more compact before gluing it on. Use craft glue.

When the glue is completely dry, dot black spots on to the sheep's wool with a felt tip pen. Run a gathering thread around the top edge of the cloak. Pull the thread until you can close the cloak under the chin.

HAIR AND CROWN

Needle-felt the hair to the head carefully but thoroughly.

To make the crown, measure the doll's head circumference and cut a length of gold braid to fit. Sew it at the back of the head with a few stitches. The crown should loosely fit the head.

SCEPTRE

To finish, paint the wooden skewer and the wooden bead with gold paint. Glue the bead to the stick once the paint is completely dry. Place it in the king's hand as a sceptre.

Queen

Make the doll according to the instructions given in the basic pattern. For exact measurements, see p.23.

DRESS

To make the dress, fold the velveteen in half, wrong sides together. Place the pattern on the velveteen and pin it in place. Velveteen is difficult to sew, so I always sew it before cutting it out. Draw around the pattern with a pencil and then pin the fabric together outside the pattern before removing the paper pattern. Sew the side seams. Then cut the dress out.

Before turning the dress right side out, cut into the fabric under the arms 3–4 times to stop the seam puckering. Smooth the seams well. The velvet will not fray so you don't need to hem the edges.

PETTICOAT

The petticoat gives the dress more volume. To make it, cut a rectangle 8 x 28 cm (3 ⅛ x 11 in) out of pink craft felt. Sew the back seam with backstitch and turn the petticoat right side out. Run a gathering thread around the top edge.

Put the petticoat on your doll and pull the gathering thread to the desired length.

Put the dress on over the petticoat. Run a gathering thread around the neck opening of the dress.

Tie gold braid around the waist under the arms. Tie the gold braid around each sleeve, approximately 1 cm (⅜ in) away from the edge.

CLOAK, HAIR, CROWN, NECKLACE

Cut a rectangle, 10 x 16 cm (4 x 6 ¼ in) out of red velveteen. Make the cloak as described for the king above, but rather than closing it below the chin, sew it to the left and right of the shoulders.

Cut the wig out of fake fur and make it as described on p.16

Make the crown the same as for the king.

To finish, make the queen a necklace out of gold beads.

Princess

Make the doll according to the basic pattern. You can find the exact measurements on p.23

Blouse

Cut the blouse out of white felt, without seam allowance. Sew the sleeve and side seams. Turn the blouse right side out and put it on the doll. Now sew the back seam.

Run a gathering thread around the neck opening, pull it to the desired length and knot it tight. Run a gathering thread approximately 1 cm ($3/8$ in) from the sleeve edges, pull to the desired length and knot tight.

Dress

Cut the dress out of patterned white felt. Sew the side seams, turn the dress right side out and put it on the doll.

Run a gathering thread around the body under the arms and pull it to the desired length. You will now have a small fold on the chest. Fold it together and sew it in place with 2–3 stitches. Then sew two gold beads to the seam as buttons.

To finish, sew a thin length of gold braid to the hem, waist, neck opening and sleeve endings with small stitches.

Hair and crown

Sew small tufts of the unspun silk strand to the head with a lot of small stitches.

Make the crown in the same way as for the king.

Prince

See the instructions given for the prince on p.41.

Castle turret

Make the castle turret out of felt. Use a felt that can be shaped when wet and then dries in the shape given. You can buy it in sheets. Simply wet the felt with water, bend it into the desired shape and leave it to dry. To make the castle turret, I placed the wet sheet in a round bowl to dry over night.

Cut the castellated turret pieces out before wetting the felt.

Once the felt is dry, draw the stone outlines and the gateway with a black or grey felt tip pen. Then cut open the gates.

To finish, glue the beads to the gates as door handles, and ivy leaves to the turret.

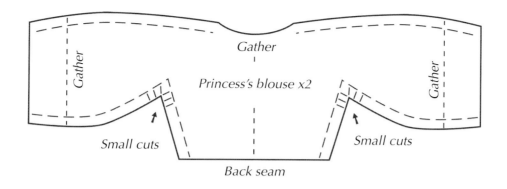

Gather

Gather

Gather

Princess's blouse x2

Small cuts

Small cuts

Back seam

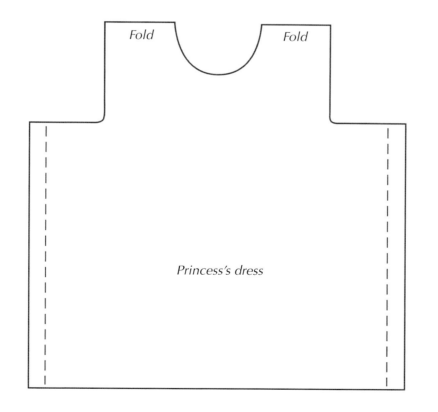

Fold

Fold

Princess's dress

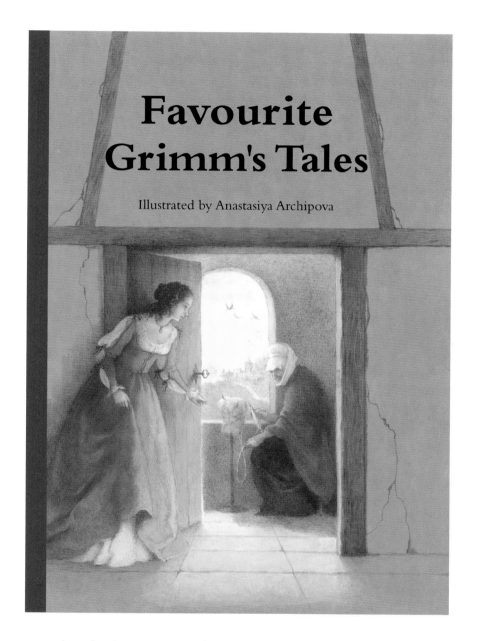

Favourite Grimm's Tales

Illustrated by Anastasiya Archipova

Almost two hundred years ago the Grimm brothers published their famous collection of folk tales, including these well-known and much loved stories.

Beautifully illustrated, this collection includes: Snow White, Rapunzel, Sleeping Beauty, Cinderella, Rumpelstiltskin, Mother Holle and many others.

Making Flower Children

Sybille Adolphi

Making More Flower Children

Sybille Adolphi

These two books contain all the patterns and instructions you will need to make your own flower children, and are clearly illustrated with diagrams and photographs throughout. Many of the figures are recognisable from Elsa Beskow's popular picture books, and from Sybille von Olfers' *The Story of the Root Children*.

Activities are organised by season, making the book ideal for decorating a nature corner or seasonal table in the home or classroom.